KT-548-452

The DETOX Cook

OVER 100 BLISSFUL DETOXING RECIPES

Louisa J Walters | Aliza Baron Cohen | Adrian Mercuri

KYLE CATHIE LIMITED

First published in Great Britain 2001 by
Kyle Cathie Limited
122 Arlington Road
London NW1 7HP
general.enquiries@kyle-cathie.com

ISBN 1 85626 404 1

All rights reserved. No reproduction, copy
or transmission of this publication may be
made without written permission. No
paragraph of this publication may be
reproduced, copied or transmitted save
with the written permission or in
accordance with the provision of the
Copyright Act 1956 (as amended). Any
person who does any unauthorised act in
relation to this publication may be liable to
criminal prosecution and civil claims for
damages.

Text © Louisa J Walters, Aliza Baron Cohen,
Adrian Mercuri 2001
Photographs © Juliet Piddington 2001

Commissioning Editor: Helen Woodhall
Editorial Assistant: Andrie Morris
Copy editor: Alexa Stace
Home Economists: Pippin Britz/Carol Tennant
Designer: Heidi Baker
Production: Sha Huxtable and Lorraine Baird

Louisa J Walters, Aliza Baron Cohen and
Adrian Mercuri are hereby identified as the
authors of this work in accordance with
Section 77 of the Copyright, Designs and
Patents Act 1988.

A Cataloguing In Publication record for this
title is available from the British Library.

Colour separations by Sang Choy, Singapore
Printed and bound in Printer Trento s.r.l.

contents

introduction

When people think of a detox, they think of suffering and the denial of good food, or even no food. The result is a very hungry, deprived and unhappy person. Not really the emotional detox one would want. As health practitioners, we tend to find that people doing these sorts of detoxes don't stick to them. This book offers a detox that is great tasting and easy to stick to. Use this simple detox diet for the rest of your life, not just for a day or a week!

We have based our relaxed and common-sense approach to detoxing on the dietary therapy of Chinese medicine, which deals with the properties of food and their effects on health and the prevention of disease. It is part of their culture for food to be a friend that is nurturing, helping to maintain and restore health. Quite the opposite from here in the West, where we tend to concentrate more on what is not good for us and become worried about what we eat, so that food becomes our enemy.

Our aim is to give a detox that does not encourage rigidity or denial. Emphasis is on listening to your body and feeding it what it needs, while still creating appetising meals – usually a daunting task when you are trying to improve your health through changes in your diet. We hope to have made this easier by helping you to determine your body type using the ancient Chinese principles of Yin and Yang (see questionnaires on page 12–13). Once you have determined if you are a hot, cold or neutral person you will be able to detox more efficiently by choosing cleansing and healthy recipes that correlate to your individual needs. This type of detox will leave you feeling healthier and more energetic than ever before.

For example, if you are a cold person and your energy is sluggish and you are always or often tired, you can correct this by eating foods from the warming recipes because they stimulate and increase the body's energy. You may have done a regular detox and eaten lots of the fruit and vegetables mentioned in the cooling recipes of this book. These would have slowed and calmed you down, making you feel even more tired and sluggish.

As holistic practitioners and chefs, we have first hand knowledge of the benefits our clients have gained when their diet reflects their lifestyle and body type. If you are sick, you need to consult a professional Chinese doctor for guidance in determining your body type, as food is not a substitute for medicine, though it can be a help.

WHY SHOULD I DETOX?

The human body is built to cope with a certain amount of toxins and has its own natural methods of eliminating excess waste. However, there is a difference between an acceptable level of toxic accumulation and a level that leads to ill health. Toxins can be formed by the faulty digestion of protein and fat, which can occur when the liver is not functioning optimally. You can stimulate digestion by eating the right foods for your body type, which will promote proper protein and fat breakdown. The recipes in this book are specifically designed to increase enzyme release that aid good digestion, as well as facilitate the elimination of waste products from the body.

Elimination of harmful toxins will leave you feeling great and bursting with energy, giving a healthy glow to your skin, hair, teeth and nails. If you frequently have no energy or less energy than you used to have and your skin is spotty and your hair dull, or you are constantly getting colds, flu, headaches and allergies, you probably need to detox. A lot of the health problems that we suffer from are due to excessive use or abuse of foods, drink, drugs and pollutants. In large quantities these become toxic to the body, clogging the tissues and suffocating the cells. The result is a decrease in energy and a weaker immune system.

The way we live today provides lots of opportunities for overindulgence in social situations, for example, at dinner parties, while clubbing with friends, and at the local pub. An excess of alcohol, nicotine, coffee, tea, sweets, chocolate, sugar, too many fatty foods, and social drugs often starts as a social habit and soon turns into a regular pastime. If we overindulge in these things, we can never feel healthy all the time.

All ancient cultures have traditionally practised detoxification processes as an important part of their lifestyle. The practices outlined in this book provide a solid foundation with which to continue this tradition into our lives today. All the recipes hold to the principle that what we eat should not only be nutritious and healthy but should also help to promote detoxification and cleansing by stimulating and toning the body's channels of elimination via the skin, kidneys, bowels and lungs.

HOW DO I DETOX AND NOT FEEL MISERABLE?

The first step to improving your health and beginning your detox is to cut out the habits that cause toxins. If you find this difficult, even cutting down or taking a week's break would be of great benefit. This will help to cleanse the body and enhance the elimination of toxins.

Some people do experience side effects or reactions such as cold sores, spots and headaches when toxins are reduced or released. To support this process drink plenty of water, take lots of exercise and multivitamin supplements. If the reaction is too uncomfortable or an illness such as a skin condition gets progressively worse, consult a health care professional.

The second step is to start replacing bad habits with ones that promote good health. Exercise regularly, especially when stressed, drink lots of water instead of coffee or tea and snack on fruits and juices – you'll be surprised at how tasty a good juice is!

Most of our recipes avoid dairy and wheat products where possible as these are the two most common triggers for allergies and intolerances in people's diets. But we know that you'll find our recipes as delicious and naughty-feeling as the foods you are used to eating, and the best bit about it all is that you'll feel great after eating them. In fact, if we hadn't told you they were from a detox menu, you would probably have felt guilty for eating them!

WHAT IS TRADITIONAL CHINESE MEDICINE (TCM)?
TCM talks about the fundamental aspects in all healthy beings as the harmonious balance between opposing yet interrelated principles. These principles, often labelled Yin and Yang, represent the duality of nature that combine to make it a whole.

The familiar Yin/Yang diagram represents the duality of life. The Yin darkness slowly turns into the Yang light and the Yang lightness slowly turns into the Yin dark. In the Yin phenomenon there is a little Yang and in the Yang, a little Yin. The Yang label represents the active, masculine, thermally *hot* quality of all things in life. The Yin represents its passive, feminine or *cold* quality.

To understand one aspect of the pair you need to consider its opposite. Thus night exists in relation to day to create time; left is relative to right to signify direction; up to down to represent height; and hot to cold to represent temperature.

HOT AND COLD BODY TYPES
The Yin/Yang phenomenon relates to body type in the form of the body's thermal nature. The Yang or Hot qualities that apply to our personality and constitution are, for example, being prone to having a warm body and dry skin; an outgoing personality and a loud voice; a red complexion; a focused, logical mentality and a more aggressive, masculine

manner. Conversely, the Yin or Cold qualities are a cooler body and moist skin; a pale complexion; an introverted personality; a serene, intuitive mentality and a more timid and passive, feminine manner.

The terms 'masculine' and 'feminine' do not denote sexual gender but are aspects within all of us. Most people fluctuate between these two aspects. Fundamentally though, one is constitutionally more Yin than Yang or vice versa.

THE THERMAL NATURE OF FOOD

Just as people have a certain thermal nature, so does food. The effect of food on the body once it has been digested has a certain energetic property, which may cause a change in body temperature. Thus we can talk about ' warming' or 'cooling' foods. There are also foods classed as neither warming or cooling which are 'neutral'.

Cooling foods direct energy inwards and downwards, primarily cooling the upper and outer parts of the body. Warming foods move energy upwards and outwards from the centre of the body to its extremities. Warm foods are said to speed us up and cool foods are said to slow us down.

WARMING FOODS
- *Vegetables:* carrot, leek, onion, shallot, spring onion, watercress
- *Fruit:* apricot, blackberry, blackcurrant, cherry, mango, strawberry, peach, quince
- *Grains, pulses, legumes:* oats, lentils, quinoa
- *Seeds and nuts:* pumpkin, sesame, sunflower and watermelon seeds, chestnuts, walnuts
- *Herbs and spices:* basil, bay leaf, caraway seeds, cardamom, chives, cinnamon, cloves, coriander leaves and seeds, cumin, dill, fennel seeds, fenugreek, garlic, ginger, lemongrass, mustard, nutmeg, oregano, pepper, spearmint, star anise

COOLING FOODS
- *Vegetables:* broccoli, cauliflower, zucchini, sweetcorn, asparagus, button mushrooms, radish, lettuce, cucumber, celery, Swiss chard, aubergine, spinach, summer squash, cabbage, bok choi
- *Fruit:* watermelon, apple, tomato, all citrus fruits, persimmons, cantaloupe, banana, pear, coconut, pineapple
- *Grains, pulses, legumes:* soya milk, soya sprouts, tofu, tempe, mung beans and their sprouts, alfalfa sprouts, barley, millet, wheat and wheat products, amaranth
- *Herbs and spices:* peppermint tea, dandelion tea, nettle tea, lemon balm tea, white peppercorns, marjoram, tarragon, turmeric
- *Others:* kelp and seaweed, wheat grass, spirulina, barley grass, yogurt, crab meat, clams

NEUTRAL FOODS
- *Vegetables:* beetroot, Brussels sprouts, fennel, parsnips, pumpkin, runner beans, snow peas, squash, swede, sweet potato, taro, turnip, yam
- *Fruit:* date, fig, grape, guava, papaya, plum, raspberry
- *Grains, pulses, legumes:* brown rice, rye, sweetcorn, aduki beans, haricot beans, peas, red kidney beans
- *Seeds and nuts:* almonds, peanuts (fresh in shells), pine nuts, raisins
- *Herbs and spices:* parsley, rosemary, sage, thyme

OTHER TYPES OF DETOX
There is a wide range of detox diets available, many of which promote very little choice of food. They range from one or three day fasts, to months at a time. We recommend that some of these fasts should not be done while working as they are not conducive to normal life and often leave people feeling exhausted. Detoxes based on Chinese principles do not advocate food deprivation as it depletes energy in the stomach and spleen. The following list shows examples of fasting detoxes, but we recommend that you do not follow any of them solely on the basis of the information given here.

1. A diet of fresh fruit and vegetables and whole grains only, with lots of water to drink. Most people find this diet one of the easier of the strict detoxes to follow.

2. A diet of brown rice only, with lots of liquids such as water and herbal/green teas. People do this fast for a couple of weeks and often feel very weak. Side effects such as headaches are common.

3. A diet of purely fruit and vegetables. This helps to cleanse the digestive tract but can be difficult to stick to for any length of time and people following it say they have no energy.

4. Liquid cleanses or fasts. Juices, vegetable broths and teas are used to purify the body whilst fasting. Again, tiredness is a common side effect of this type of fast and it is not recommended that you undertake it while continuing any normal activities, such as working.

5. Water fasting is more intense than juice fasting and often results in the person feeling lethargic and lacking energy.

QUICK REFERENCE TIPS FOR HEALTHY EATING

- Choose organic produce and eat whole food with lots of fibre
- Reduce refined foods such as sugar, fatty foods, additives and colourings
- Don't drink a lot of liquid with your meals as this dilutes the digestive juices
- Chew food thoroughly
- Eat in a relaxed environment and never eat while upset or during an argument
- Eat small regular meals and don't overeat
- Drink adequate water and herbal teas daily (see water consumption opposite)
- Moderate or eliminate stimulants or drugs such as alcohol, caffeine and nicotine
- Exercise regularly

WATER CONSUMPTION

The kidneys filter large volumes of waste from the body each day. Basically, they are a highly sensitive mechanism of pumps that functions to regulate fluid balance, blood pressure and excrete metabolic toxins. Fluid intake requirements are different for each of us according to our body. With too much water, the kidneys lose their subtle function to gauge how much water the body needs. It has been a popular practice to drink at least 2¹/₂ litres (8 glasses) of water each day. According to the principles of Chinese medicine this practice will deplete the proper functioning of the kidneys to regulate fluid levels in the body. The solution calls for a level of intuition regarding how much water to consume each day. There are, however, certain key factors to remember. First and most obviously, drink according to your thirst. Secondly, it is more helpful for proper digestion to drink outside of meal times; at least 30 minutes to an hour before and after food intake. Thirdly, when drinking any fluid it is important to take small amounts at any time, rather than guzzling down a whole cup in one swig.

Once again the proper functioning of the kidneys is based on recognising subtle changes in the body's fluid level. If the kidneys are overburdened with sudden bursts of water over a short period of time their responsiveness will be less effective. You can vary the amount of water you need according to your amount of physical activity. However, hot body types generally require more water consumption than cold body types. The way to gauge exactly how much to drink is that if you begin to feel uncharacteristically more cold after water consumption, drink less. If you don't drink much water and you feel excessively hot, drink regularly but moderately to abate the feeling.

DETERMINING YOUR BODY TYPE

In order to use this book optimally you need to determine your thermal nature. In doing so you can begin to balance your diet suited to your body type and detox effectively and safely. Below are two questionnaires to determine your body type and thereby point you in the direction of the foods and recipes which will be most effective for you.

ARE YOU A HOT PERSON?	yes	no	sometimes
1. Do you often feel hot?	☐	☐	☐
2. Do you have a red or ruddy complexion?	☐	☐	☐
3. Are you often restless, impatient, excitable, or hyper?	☐	☐	☐
4. Do you talk fast and walk fast?	☐	☐	☐
5 Do you suffer from dry eyes, skin or throat?	☐	☐	☐
6. Do you have problems sleeping or getting off to sleep?	☐	☐	☐
7. Are you prone to red eyes?	☐	☐	☐
8. Are you prone to headaches?	☐	☐	☐
9. Are you always thirsty, especially for cold drinks?	☐	☐	☐
10. Do you fidget lots?	☐	☐	☐
11. Do you have a rapid heart rate?	☐	☐	☐
12. Are you prone to sudden changes in your health?	☐	☐	☐
13. Do you have dark scanty urine?	☐	☐	☐
14. Do you throw off the bed covers at night?	☐	☐	☐
15. Do you like to lie stretched out in bed?	☐	☐	☐
16. Are your arms and legs and body hot to the touch?	☐	☐	☐
17. Do you have a loud voice?	☐	☐	☐
18. Do you like to talk a lot?	☐	☐	☐
19. Is your breathing heavy and loud?	☐	☐	☐
20. Do you have skin problems (eg eczema, psoriasis)?	☐	☐	☐
Totals	☐	☐	☐

ARE YOU A COLD PERSON?

		yes	no	sometimes
1.	Do you feel the cold?	☐	☐	☐
2.	Are you a quiet person?	☐	☐	☐
3.	Do you walk slowly and talk slowly?	☐	☐	☐
4.	Are you prone to oedema or water retention?	☐	☐	☐
5.	Do you urinate often and/or with pale watery urine?	☐	☐	☐
6.	Are you often tired, sleepy or listless?	☐	☐	☐
7.	Are you prone to watery eyes and/or nose?	☐	☐	☐
8.	Do you have a slow heart rate?	☐	☐	☐
9.	Does your health change gradually?	☐	☐	☐
10.	Do you like to be covered up in bed?	☐	☐	☐
11.	Do you like to curl up in bed?	☐	☐	☐
12.	Do your arms, legs and body feel cold to the touch?	☐	☐	☐
13.	Do you prefer hot drinks?	☐	☐	☐
14.	Do you have a weak or quiet voice?	☐	☐	☐
15.	Do you dislike talking?	☐	☐	☐
16.	Do you rarely have a thirst?	☐	☐	☐
17.	Are you relaxed and easy going?	☐	☐	☐
18.	Are you vulnerable to colds?	☐	☐	☐
19.	Do you have shallow or weak breathing?	☐	☐	☐
20.	Do you prefer not to be very active?	☐	☐	☐
	Totals	☐	☐	☐

Fill out both questionnaires and add up the total for each column. If you answer mostly YES to the questions in Are you a hot person? then you should choose cooling recipes or neutral recipes. If you answer mostly YES to the questions in Are you a cold person? you should choose warming recipes or neutral recipes.

If you answer mostly SOMETIMES in both questionnaires, you are a neutral person. You can therefore have a wide variety of recipes from all the sections.

warming foods

warming foods
for cold people

Without heat, life slows down and we become cold and sluggish. Cold people dislike the cold, love the heat and are often overdressed and attracted to warm foods and drinks. Too much cold in the body can be due to many factors such as:

- **lack of physical activity**
- **eating too many cooling foods (see page 8) and/or not enough warming foods**
- **over-exposure to an extremely cold climate**
- **constitutional weakness at birth**

If you are a cold person, avoid foods that will make you feel even colder. Eat more warming foods and fewer raw and cooling foods. When you do eat cooling foods, boil, bake, pressure-cook or deep-fry to make them warmer. Don't eat food below room temperature and avoid putting ice in drinks. See page 8 for a full list of warming foods.

When warming foods are eaten, they push the blood and energy from deep inside to rise up and out to the surface of the body. If we heat ourselves up too much so that we sweat, we will lose energy when we cool down. To avoid this, balance warming foods with those from the neutral section, as they will not make you any colder. Remember that it takes longer for a cold person to create warmth than it does for a hot person to cool down. Chewing food thoroughly also creates more warmth, so a cooling food chewed thoroughly can become more warming.

SPICY ROOT SOUP

This soup is a great detoxifier, as it helps the liver, the lymphatic system, the bowel, urinary and nervous systems. Parsnips have medicinal value, and simple Chinese remedies still use them to treat coughs, colds, rheumatism and arthritis. Serves 2

1 tablespoon olive oil **1 large onion, finely chopped**	Gently fry in a pan over a low heat for 2–3 minutes, until the onion starts to soften.
1 garlic clove, crushed **1/2 teaspoon ground coriander** **1/4 teaspoon ground cinnamon** **1/2 teaspoon ground cumin** **1/4 teaspoon ground ginger** **3 cardamom pods** **Pinch of chilli powder or 2 teaspoons curry powder** **1 bay leaf**	Add to the pan and fry for another 2 minutes, until the spices start to release their aromas.
250g (9oz) parsnips, peeled and diced **170g (6oz) celeriac, peeled and diced** **300ml (1/2 pint) vegetable stock**	Add to the pan, cover and simmer for 20 minutes until the vegetables are soft.
600ml (1 pint) vegetable stock	Add and simmer for another 10 minutes.
Salt and freshly ground black pepper **Fresh coriander leaves, to garnish**	Season to taste and serve garnished.

CARROT, ORANGE AND GINGER SOUP

These ingredients are beneficial if you have a hangover or feel as if you are beginning to get a cold. The orange in this soup is an excellent source of water-soluble vitamin C. Ginger helps to push out a cold or fever and is good for relieving the discomfort of diarrhoea, stomach gas and gout. Serves 2

1 medium onion, finely chopped, **3 medium carrots, peeled and finely** **sliced** **340ml (12fl oz) water**	Place in a large pan, bring to the boil and simmer for 15 minutes, until the carrots are soft.
5cm (2 in) root ginger, peeled and **finely grated**	Gather all the bits into your hand and squeeze the juice into the soup. Discard the ginger fibre.
340ml (12fl oz) water **Zest of ½ orange** **Juice of 1 orange** **Pinch of sea salt** **Freshly ground black pepper**	Add to the pan, bring back to the boil and simmer for another 10 minutes.
Chopped chives, to garnish	Add to the pan then remove from the heat. Blend in a food processor or liquidiser until smooth. Reheat and serve garnished.

PUMPKIN, PORCINI AND FRESH DILL SOUP

The pumpkin in this soup helps the spleen, stomach and kidneys. Its nutrients are known to calm a hyperactive foetus, so this is a good soup to eat during the last trimester of pregnancy. Dill is a stimulant for the liver's detoxing function. It helps to prevent stomach gas and the accumulation of food residue in the intestines. Serves 2

20g (³/₄ oz) dried porcini mushrooms **150ml (¹/₄ pint) boiling water**	Place in a bowl and leave to soak.
1 onion, chopped **1 garlic clove** **100ml (3¹/₂ fl oz) vegetable stock**	Sweat in a pan, covered, until the onion is soft, about 10 minutes.
50g (2oz) fresh mushrooms, sliced **250g (9oz) pumpkin, peeled, seeded and diced** **¹/₄ teaspoon dried thyme** **1 teaspoon dried sage** **Pinch of grated nutmeg** **1 dessertspoon soy sauce** **250ml (9fl oz) vegetable stock**	Add to the pan, cover and simmer for 10 minutes, or until the pumpkin is tender.
	Drain the porcini mushrooms, reserving the water, and add them to the pan. Strain the water through a sieve with a kitchen towel to remove any grit.
Freshly ground black pepper **1 tablespoon fresh dill weed, chopped** **250ml (9fl oz) vegetable stock**	Add to the soup with the porcini liquid and simmer for 5 minutes. This soup can be served as it is or liquidised for a creamy texture.

MISO AND GINGER SOUP

Miso is rich, yet subtle in flavour and extremely good for you. It is made from soya beans, which can lower the risk of heart disease. It also reduces menopausal symptoms and is thought to help prevent cancer. Together with ginger, this soup aids digestion, helps prevent nausea and is good for sweating out a cold.
Serves 2

100ml (3¹/₂ fl oz) vegetable stock	Heat in a pan.
2 medium onions, sliced into half moons **1 garlic clove, crushed** **2 tablespoons very thinly sliced ginger** **1¹/₂ teaspoons dried sage**	Add to the pan. Cover and simmer for 5 minutes.
2 tablespoons brown miso **1 carrot, sliced in rounds** **800ml (1¹/₃ pints) vegetable stock**	Add to the pan. Cover and simmer for 20 minutes or until the vegetables are soft. Serve immediately.

TOM KA KAI

The chicken in this soup is an energy tonic. It helps the kidneys, spleen and stomach because it is good for digestion, poor appetite and diarrhoea. It also builds up the blood, making it good for palpitations and anaemia. Coconut milk is a complete protein food that strengthens the body, so is very good to drink during convalescence. Serves 4

850ml (1 pint 9fl oz) coconut milk **450ml (³/₄ pint) chicken stock**	Bring to the boil in a large pan.
1 small red chilli, left whole but pricked with a knife **4 stems lemongrass** **2.5 cm (1in) galangal, or root ginger** **¹/₄ teaspoon ground black pepper** **6 kaffir lime leaves**	Add to the pan and simmer for 20 minutes.
1 chicken breast, boned, skinned and cut into strips **100g (3¹/₂ oz) shiitake or button mushrooms**	Add to the pan and simmer for a further 10 minutes or until the chicken is cooked yet tender. Remove the spices with a slotted spoon.
2 spring onions, chopped **4 tablespoons lime juice** **Pinch of sea salt, optional** **Fresh coriander, to garnish**	Add, and serve garnished with coriander.

RAW YANG PURITY

In a balanced diet, it is important to alternate the consumption of raw foods with the consumption of cooked foods. The warming vegetables and herbal ingredients in this all-raw dish will help to circulate blood around the body, give support and comfort the detoxing organs.

coriander leaf
mustard greens
onion
parsley
kale
leek
parsnip
pepper
spring onion
celeriac
watercress

There are no strict measurements as the idea is that you can make a very quick and simple salad using whatever you have available in your food store, and that the quantities can be varied to give a different taste each time you make it.

This is the essence of detox, and this recipe should become a staple, being eaten as a snack and/or with meals.

It is best made using a hand mincer, but a processor will do. Wash the vegetables and roughly chop them. Put them in the processor and blend until everything is chopped very finely. Turn into a bowl and serve. You can squeeze some fresh lemon juice over the salad to prevent browning if you wish. It will keep in the fridge for no more than a day.

ADUKI AND HARICOTS WITH CREAMED AVOCADO DRESSING

Aduki beans detoxify by removing swelling and water accumulation in the lower region of the body. They also tone up the heart and spleen by promoting the flow of fluids. Avocado contains fourteen minerals that regulate the body's functions and stimulate the growth of skin, hair, teeth and nails. Its copper and iron content aids red blood regeneration and improves energy levels. Serves 2

FOR THE DRESSING

1 avocado, stoned and peeled
juice of 1/2 lemon
2 tablespoons water
1/2 teaspoon paprika
Dash of tabasco sauce
Pinch of salt

Place in a liquidiser or food processor and blend to a smooth creamy texture.

220g (7oz) tin of kidney beans, drained and rinsed
220g (7oz) tin of aduki beans, drained and rinsed
1 stick celery, chopped
1 apple, chopped
1 spring onion, chopped
4 cherry tomatoes, halved
5 basil leaves, torn into pieces
1 handful chopped chives

Place in a salad bowl, mix well together and pour over the dressing. Toss well and serve.

CYPRIOT SALAD

Haloumi is a tasty salty cheese made from sheep's milk. It doesn't have the allergic effects of cow's milk cheese because the size of its protein particles enables better digestion. Serves 2

50g (2oz) haloumi cheese, cut into 5mm (¹/₄ in) slices, then diced

Toast under a medium grill on a non-stick baking sheet until golden brown. Turn once and brown the other side.

4 medium tomatoes
¹/₄ cucumber, sliced
¹/₄ yellow pepper, cored, seeded and diced
1 handful of flat-leaf parsley, roughly chopped
10 black olives, stoned
¹/₂ red onion, thinly sliced
3–4 large lettuce leaves, torn into pieces

Mix with the cheese in a salad bowl.

FOR THE DRESSING
2 tablespoons extra-virgin olive oil
1 tablespoon white wine vinegar
1–2 teaspoons lemon juice
Pinch of sea salt
Freshly ground black pepper

Mix well and pour over the salad. Toss well.

VALENCIANA

Rice strengthens the spleen and pancreas by expelling toxins from the body. It is a tropical grain that is thought to soothe people who get irritable when the weather is very hot. The Chinese feed rice to those with a poor appetite and weak digestion. It is also given to nursing mothers who have painful, swollen breasts. Serves 2

125g (4½ oz) brown rice

Place in a pan with enough water and boil until tender. Drain and leave to cool, then transfer to a salad bowl.

2 spring onions, chopped
1 tablespoon pine nuts, toasted
until golden
5 cherry tomatoes, cut in half
8 black olives, stoned and halved
1 small handful raisins
1 tablespoon chopped parsley
2 teaspoons tomato purée
1 teaspoon soy sauce
1 teaspoon vinegar

Add to the rice, mix well and serve.

ROAST PEPPER AND BASIL DIP

This protective dish uses sweet peppers, which contain vitamins A, B and C. There is as much vitamin C in peppers as there is in oranges, making them good for building up resistance to colds and flu. Basil is a warming energy-giving herb that induces sweating and harmonises the stomach, to aid gentle digestion.
Serves 2

Preheat the oven to 200°C/400°F/gas mark 6.

1 large red pepper

Roast on a baking tray in the centre of the oven for 20–30 minutes, or until the skin goes black. Remove from the oven and leave to cool. Peel off the skin and seed and core, saving any juice.

100ml (4fl oz) soya milk
½ teaspoon paprika
½ teaspoon salt
2 teaspoons extra-virgin olive oil
2 teaspoons cider vinegar
1 tablespoon chopped basil

Place in a liquidiser or food processor with the pepper flesh and juice and blend to a smooth creamy texture.

Serve chilled as a dip or warm as a sauce for other dishes.

SALADS and SNACKS

BEETROOT, ROCKET, APPLE AND CASHEW NUT SALAD

This is a powerful, mineral-rich meal. The high iron content in beetroot helps to purify the blood and promote menstruation. It also strengthens the heart and sedates the spirit. Cashews are a good source of magnesium, helping to reduce incidence of osteoarthritis. Apples cleanse the body and protect against disease-producing bacteria in the gut. Serves 2

1 large or 2 small fresh beetroot, peeled and finely chopped **1 dessert apple, finely chopped** **2 large handfuls fresh rocket, washed and chopped**	Place in a salad bowl.
25g (1oz) cashew nuts, chopped	Place on a baking sheet under the grill on medium heat, and toast until golden brown. Turn once or twice to brown all sides.
1 carrot, peeled	With a vegetable peeler, cut thick shavings of carrot. Add to the bowl with the cashew nuts and mix well.
FOR THE DRESSING **1 dessertspoon extra-virgin olive oil** **3 dessertspoons fresh lemon juice** **Pinch of sea salt** **Freshly ground black pepper**	Mix and pour over the salad immediately before serving.

TERRINE OF FENNEL, BRAZIL NUT AND SAGE

Sage is a highly antiseptic and rejuvenating herb that can help fight off infection. It improves the immune system, stimulates digestion and eases liver complaints. Ancient Greeks called sage the 'immortal herb' and the Egyptians praised it as a lifesaver, hence its botanical name *Salvia*, meaning to save. Serves 2

Preheat the oven to 190°C/375°F/gas mark 5.

170g (6oz) brazil nuts

Place on a baking tray and roast in the oven for 10 minutes until golden brown. Leave to cool, then place them in a liquidiser or food processor and process until they are finely chopped.

1 teaspoon extra-virgin olive oil
1 fennel bulb, finely chopped
1 small onion, finely chopped
1/2 teaspoon fennel seeds

Place in a pan, covered, and sweat for 6–7 minutes.

7–8 button mushrooms, finely chopped
1 tablespoon sage leaves or 1 teaspoon dried

Add to the pan, cover and sweat for another 5 minutes, until the mushrooms start to release their juices.

Freshly ground black pepper
1 tablespoon soy sauce

Add to the nuts with the vegetable mixture and process to a rough paste.

Turn into a small greased loaf tin, press down evenly, and cover with a piece of greaseproof paper to prevent it drying out. Bake for 20 minutes.

This dish goes well with a simple tomato sauce, such as the sauce for butterbean and coriander potato cakes (see page 73).

MARINATED PRAWNS WITH SWEET PEPPERS AND TOASTED SESAME SEEDS

Some Chinese studies show that sesame lowers blood sugar levels. Research has also shown that garlic can be used as a treatment for numerous health problems including gastritis, dysentery and constipation. Ginger rids the body of toxins, aids digestion and helps soothe nausea. Serves 2

200g (7oz) cooked prawns
1 small garlic clove, crushed
1cm (1/2 in) root ginger, peeled
    and grated
1/2 teaspoon garam masala
1/4 teaspoon turmeric
1/4 red chilli, seeded and finely
    chopped
2 dessertspoons lemon juice

Mix in a bowl and leave to marinate for 1 hour.

1/2 red pepper, cored, seeded and
    thinly sliced
1 spring onion, chopped
1 small handful of fresh beansprouts
2 teaspoons sesame seeds, toasted

Add to the bowl, mix well and serve immediately. A rice salad or other grain dish would complement this salad.

STEAMED CITRUS MUSSELS

Mussels strengthen the liver and kidneys and are an important remedy for raising the body's energy levels. They also help regulate menstruation and stimulate the process of semen production. Serves 2

1 garlic clove, crushed

1cm (½ in) root ginger, peeled and finely sliced

2 stems fresh lemongrass, outer leaves removed and finely chopped

50 ml (2fl oz) rice wine vinegar or white wine vinegar

50 ml (2fl oz) dry white wine (optional) or water

Juice of ½ lemon

Place in a large pan, bring to the boil and simmer for 5 minutes.

1.2kg (2lb) fresh mussels, well scrubbed

Add to the pan, cover with a lid and cook over a low heat for 3–4 minutes, shaking the pan occasionally.

75ml (3 fl oz) coconut milk
Juice of 1 lime

Add when the mussels are open, cover and shake once or twice to coat all the mussels in the sauce. Discard any mussels which are not open and serve immediately.

RED DRAGON PIE

Potatoes are anti-viral, anti-inflammatory and can help digestion. Recent research has found that they contain certain properties that may be effective against cancer. The antioxidant quality of the skin helps a variety of degenerative diseases. Ancient Chinese people believed that potatoes could even relieve the toxic symptoms of chicken pox. Serves 2

Preheat the oven to 200°C/400°F/gas mark 6.

125g (4¹⁄₂ oz) aduki beans, soaked for 8 hours and drained	Boil in plenty of water for 10 minutes, then reduce the heat and simmer for 40 minutes or until tender.
1 large potato, diced	Boil until tender and drain.
1 teaspoon sesame seeds **1 dessertspoon soya milk**	Add to the potatoes and mash together.
1 teaspoon extra-virgin olive oil **1 medium onion, finely chopped**	Place in a pan and fry gently, covered, for 5 minutes, until the onion is softened.
¹⁄₂ red pepper, cored, seeded and cut into strips **¹⁄₂ green pepper, cored, seeded and cut into strips** **1 teaspoon paprika**	Add to the pan and fry, covered, for another 5 minutes.

½ **teaspoon dried basil**

3 **dessertspoons tomato purée**

2 **dessertspoons brown miso**

1 **dessertspoon soy sauce**

150ml (¼ **pint) water**

Add to the pan, bring to the boil then simmer very gently for 15 minutes.

When the beans are cooked, drain and add to the sauce, stirring them in well. Turn into an ovenproof dish, and top with the mashed potatoes. Bake in the oven for 25 minutes, until bubbling and browned on top.

BAKED MUSHROOMS STUFFED WITH OLIVES AND WALNUTS

Mushrooms contain germanium, which increases oxygen efficiency in the body, counteracts the effects of pollutants and increases resistance to disease. They are also a good source of vitamin B. Olives quench thirst and promote the flow of body fluids. Serves 2

Preheat the oven to 190°C/375°F/gas mark 5.

4 large flat mushrooms

Remove the stalks and reserve.

100g (4oz) olives, stoned

100g (4oz) walnuts

1 tablespoon chopped parsley

Place in a liquidiser or food processor with the mushroom stalks. Blend until all the nuts are broken down and the mixture is quite paste-like.

Divide the mixture between the mushrooms, and push evenly into each cavity. Place on a non-stick baking sheet and bake in the centre of the oven for 20–25 minutes, until the mushroom flesh is succulent and cooked. Serve hot.

GINGER, ADUKI BEAN AND CELERIAC CAKES

Ginger sweats out colds and flu. It can also speed up blood circulation and aids digestion to create feelings of general well-being. Celeriac is packed full of useful nutrients that are effective for maintaining the lymphatic system and preventing the onset of arthritic ailments. Serves 2

400g (14oz) celeriac, peeled and cut into cubes **250g (9oz) potato, peeled and cut into cubes**	Boil until tender, drain and reserve.
2 teaspoons extra-virgin olive oil **1 small onion, finely chopped**	Gently fry for 5 minutes, until the onion is soft.
½ teaspoon ground coriander **½ teaspoon ground cumin** **½ teaspoon paprika** **½ teaspoon ground cinnamon** **1 teaspoon dried thyme**	Add to the pan and cook for another 5 minutes.
2 teaspoon soy sauce **400g (14oz) can aduki beans, drained and rinsed**	Place in a bowl with the potatoes and celeriac, add the onion mixture and mash well together.
1 tablespoon plain flour **1 tablespoon extra-virgin olive oil**	Form into burger shapes and coat with a little flour. Oil a heavy-based frying pan and heat over a medium flame. Fry the burgers until they are golden brown, turn and cook the other side.

warming foods

ROASTED PUMPKIN STUFFED WITH MUSHROOM AND GARLIC

The antiseptic and antioxidant action of garlic cleanses the liver and drives away infection. Pumpkins are high in potassium and sodium and are a good source of vitamins B and C. They benefit the spleen and stomach and stabilise a hyperactive foetus. Serves 2

Preheat the oven to 200°C/400°F/gas mark 6.

1 small orange pumpkin

Slice the top off and scoop out the seeds, reserving the top.

1 teaspoon extra-virgin olive oil
1 small onion, finely chopped

Place in a small pan and fry gently, covered, for 5–6 minutes, until the onion is softened.

2 garlic cloves, crushed
1 teaspoon dried mixed herbs
1/2 teaspoon black mustard seeds

Add to the pan and fry for 1 minute, until the mustard seeds start to pop.

150g (5oz) button mushrooms, finely chopped

Add to the pan, cover and sweat for 5–10 minutes until cooked.

Pinch of sea salt

Season, then fill the pumpkin with the mushroom mixture and put the top on. Stand the pumpkin in a small ovenproof dish, supported with cocktail sticks if necessary. Bake in the oven for 50–60 minutes, until the flesh is soft.

To serve, remove the top and slice into halves or quarters.

ANDEAN QUINOA AND VEGETABLE STEW

Quinoa is a high-protein cereal that strengthens the energising functions of the whole body. It also contains even more calcium than milk and is a very good source of iron and vitamins B and E. Serves 2

25g (1oz) brazil nuts, broken in half	Roast or grill for 5–10 minutes until golden, then reserve.
125g (4¹/₂oz) quinoa **300ml (¹/₂ pint) water**	Place in a pan, bring to the boil and simmer for 10–15 minutes until tender, strain and reserve.
1 tablespoon extra-virgin olive oil **1 medium onion, finely chopped**	Gently fry in a covered pan for 5–6 minutes, until the onion is softened.
1 teaspoon ground cumin **1 teaspoon ground coriander** **1 red chilli, seeded and finely chopped**	Add to the pan and fry for a further minute.
1 celery stalk, finely chopped **1 carrot, sliced** **1 medium potato, diced** **¹/₂ red pepper, cored, seeded and cut into strips** **1 tablespoon water**	Add to the pan. Cover and sweat for 5–10 minutes over a low heat.
400g (14oz) can chopped tomatoes **1 teaspoon dried oregano** **Pinch of sea salt**	Add, cover and simmer gently for a further 10 minutes, until the stew is thickened.
	Add the nuts and quinoa to the stew and simmer very gently for 3–4 minutes until well mixed and evenly heated. Serve immediately.

PEACH AND MANGO CRUMBLE

A yummy dessert that is also good for detoxing – is that possible? Peaches benefit the stomach and large intestine channels. They promote blood circulation and the flow of body fluids, thereby moistening dryness and remedying constipation. The sweet and sour qualities of mangoes quench thirst. They settle the stomach and encourage digestion. Serves 2

Preheat the oven to 190°C/375°F/gas mark 5.

1 peach, quartered
1 mango, peeled and cut into chunks
200ml (8fl oz) unsweetened apple juice

Place in a pan and simmer very gently for 15 minutes until the fruit is tender and the juice has reduced and thickened. Transfer to an ovenproof dish.

75g (3oz) oats
25g (1oz) soya margarine
2 teaspoons honey
2 teaspoons sesame seeds
25g (1oz) chopped almonds

Mix together with your fingers until the oats are coated with the fat and honey.

Spread the oat crumble topping over the fruit and bake in the oven for 20 minutes until golden brown.

Serve hot with cashew cream (see page 80).

YANG FRUIT COMPOTE

This stewed fruit concoction contains minerals, vitamins, enzymes and fibre, making it easily digestible and cleansing. Cherries are often used to improve the blood and to treat anaemia. Cinnamon is a potent antiseptic that warms the whole system. In summer, it can be served as a simple fruit salad. Serves 2

10 blackberries

10 cherries

4 dried figs, chopped

1 peach, stoned and chopped

2 apricots, stoned and chopped

$\frac{1}{4}$ teaspoon ground cinnamon

2 tablespoons apple juice

Place in a pan and simmer very gently for 20 minutes, until the juices are released and the fruit is tender. Serve warm.

SPICED BROWN RICE PUDDING

Brown rice is full of B vitamins and is therefore excellent for the nervous system, helping to relieve depression. Rice soothes the stomach, strengthens the spleen and pancreas, increases energy and expels toxins. Rice pudding is very therapeutic; the longer it is cooked, the more therapeutic it becomes. Serves 2

	Preheat the oven to 180°C/350°F/gas mark 4.
600ml (1 pint) water	Bring to the boil in a large pan.
150g (5 $^1/_2$ oz) short-grain brown rice	Add and simmer for 15 minutes. The rice should be half-cooked. Strain and return to the pan.
300ml ($^1/_2$ pint) soya milk **2 tablespoons rice syrup or date syrup** **$^1/_2$ teaspoon ground cinnamon** **$^1/_8$ nutmeg, grated** **2 whole cloves** **1 small handful of raisins** **2 shavings of orange peel**	Add to the pan and bring to the boil, then simmer very gently for 20 minutes.
Soya milk (if required)	Turn the rice into a very lightly greased ovenproof dish, cover with a lid or foil and bake in the centre of the oven for 40 minutes, until the rice is very tender. Add more soya milk if the rice begins to look dry. Serve with chopped fruit such as bananas or mangoes.

FRESH FRUIT CAKE

Oats contain B vitamins, making them an excellent body builder. Their soothing quality allows them to strengthen the stomach and spleen and tone up the chi. Oats are a natural agent which are high in fibre, and because they can be digested quickly, they pass easily into the colon and help to destroy the putrefactive poisons caused by the decomposition of other foods. Serves 2

Preheat the oven to 180°C/350°F/gas mark 4.

425g (15oz) chopped fresh fruit, such as peach, blackberry, raspberry, date, cherry or plum
225g (8oz) oats
225g (8oz) plain flour
85g (3oz) dessicated coconut
225ml (8fl oz) sunflower oil
310ml (11fl oz) unsweetened fruit juice
1¹/₂ tablespoons date syrup
140g (5oz) raisins

Mix all together in a large bowl.

Turn into a 23cm (9in) non-stick cake tin. Bake in the centre of the oven for 45 minutes, until brown and firm to the touch. Cool on a wire rack.

HOT FIGS IN A GINGER AND PLUM SAUCE

In Chinese medicine, figs are known as 'bright vision fruit' because the carotene in them helps our ability to see in dim light. They are also great energy providers and are eaten as a stomach tonic. Plums are good for the liver and stomach because they promote the production of digestive fluids. Serves 2

6–7 red plums, halved, stoned and sliced

2 tablespoons rice syrup or maple syrup

¹/₂ teaspoon ground ginger

Heat in a pan, stirring to prevent it burning.

Juice of ¹/₂ lemon

As the plums begin to soften and liquefy, add the lemon juice and bring to the boil. Cook for a few minutes, stirring continuously, until the sauce thickens.

Push the sauce through a fine sieve, to remove any pieces of plum skin. Return to the pan and keep warm over a very low heat.

6 fresh or canned figs

2 tablespoons apple juice

Heat in a pan and cover until the apple juice comes to the boil. Reduce the heat and simmer very gently for 2–3 minutes to heat the figs through – they do not need to be cooked.

Arrange the figs on serving plates and pour over the sauce. Serve hot, with a little cashew cream (see page 80).

warming foods

BREAKFAST MUESLI

Seeds are a high protein food, containing more protein than grains. They are concentrated sources of vitamins B, D and E, the minerals calcium, magnesium, iron and zinc. This makes them an ideal energy and vitality enriching food.

6 parts oats
1 part linseeds
1 part desiccated coconut
1 part pine nuts
1/2 part walnuts
1 part sunflower seeds
3 parts dried dates, chopped

You can make up as much muesli in advance as you wish, and keep it in an airtight container.

blackberries
cherries
soya milk

Serve with soya milk, topped with the fresh fruit. Soak the muesli in the soya milk for 10–20 minutes before serving.

warming foods

CARROT, APPLE AND GINGER JUICE

The antioxidant quality of carrot and ginger makes this a great anti-ageing juice. It is also a great remedy for the onset of a cold or flu and for nausea, morning and travel sickness. Carrot cleanses the digestive tract and detoxifies the liver. Apples contain pectin, which binds to toxic metals such as mercury and lead and carries them out of the body. Serves 1

3–4 large carrots
2 dessert apples
Piece of ginger 1cm x 1cm ($\frac{1}{2}$ in x $\frac{1}{2}$ in)

Take the tops off the carrots and quarter the apples, there is no need to peel anything.

Push all ingredients through a juicing machine, serve immediately.

APPLE, CINAMMON AND CLOVE JUICE

This is great to drink when you feel a cold coming on, or simply feel under the weather. Cinammon warms the whole system and cloves have natural anaethetic qualities. Serves 1

3 dessert apples

Quarter and push through the juicing machine.
Warm the apple juice gently in a pan, without boiling.

4 cloves

Add to juice in pan, then pour juice into tall glass.

$\frac{1}{2}$ teaspoon ground cinnamon

Add to juice in glass and serve immediately.

neutral foods

neutral foods

If a person is not clearly hot or cold, then a diet balanced in warming, cooling and neutral properties is best. As a neutral person you can eat all the delicious recipes from all the sections to try and remain as balanced as possible. See page 8 for a list of neutral foods. As a hot or cold person you can eat recipes from this section as well as recipes from the appropriate section for your body type.

TOMATO BISQUE

Tomatoes help to clear heat, and are great thirst-quenchers. Sweet peppers are a good source of beta-carotene, iron and potassium, which protect and build a strong immune system. Parsley contains more vitamin C than many citrus fruits, helping the body to defend itself against harmful bacteria. Serves 2

8 large fresh tomatoes, roughly chopped	Blend in a liquidiser or food processor and reserve.
1 teaspoon extra-virgin olive oil **1 small onion, finely chopped**	Place in a large pan, cover, and sweat for 10 minutes, until the onions are golden.
1 dessertspoon tomato purée	Add to the onions with the pulped tomatoes, bring to the boil and simmer for 10 minutes uncovered.
600ml (1 pint) vegetable stock **1 dessertspoon soy sauce**	Add to the pan and simmer for 10 minutes.
1 tablespoon chopped basil **Juice of ½ lemon**	Add to the pan, simmer for another 2 minutes and serve.

LENTIL AND CARROT SOUP

This easily digestible no-fuss soup provides a rich mineral supply to the whole body. Lentils are high in magnesium, potassium, phosphorous and manganese – all extremely beneficial for the proper functioning of the muscular and nervous systems. Carrots expel toxins from the bladder and bowels. They are also useful for liver and kidney problems. Serves 2

1 teaspoon extra-virgin olive oil **1 medium onion, finely chopped** **1 stick celery, finely chopped**	Place in a large pan and sweat gently, covered, for 5 minutes, until the onions are soft.
1 large carrot, peeled and sliced **2 tomatoes, skinned and chopped** **1 small garlic clove, crushed** **1 bay leaf** **1 teaspoon ground coriander** **$1/2$ teaspoon ground cumin**	Add to the pan, cover, and sweat gently for another 10 minutes, until the carrot starts to soften.
125g (4$1/2$oz) puy lentils, soaked for 12 hours and drained **700ml (1$1/4$ pints) vegetable stock or water**	Add to the pan and bring to the boil. Simmer covered for about 1 hour, until the lentils are very tender.
1 tablespoon soy sauce	Add to the pan when the lentils are tender.
Chopped parsley, to garnish	Serve garnished.

SPICED GAZPACHO

Tomatoes are used to treat anorexia and acts as a liver stimulant to help eliminate toxins. They are rich in beta-carotene and lycopene, two anti-cancer nutrients, and together with chilli, this soup cleanses the lungs. Cultures that use chilli in their diets have a low incidence of respiratory problems. Serves 2

$1/2$ **small cucumber**
450g (1lb) good quality fresh tomatoes
$1/2$ **red onion**
$1/2$ **yellow pepper, cored and seeded**
1 garlic clove, crushed
1 red chilli, seeded and finely chopped
1 small handful of parsley
1 small handful of coriander
1 dessertspoon extra-virgin olive oil
Pinch of sea salt
Pinch of paprika
Freshly ground black pepper
1 tablespoon cider vinegar

Parsley and coriander leaves, to garnish

Place all ingredients in a food processor and blend until they are well chopped, but not puréed.

Serve at room temperature, garnished.

CHESTNUT, CHICKPEA AND DILL SOUP

Of all nuts, chestnuts are the lowest in fat. Their sweetness complements the delicate flavour of aromatic spices like dill, which has a cleansing effect on the liver. In small amounts, dill stimulates the energy of the body and removes stagnant energy. It also has a very calming effect on digestion and the mind.

Serves 2

200g (7oz) dried chickpeas, soaked overnight, then drained and rinsed
1.2 litres (2 pints) water
Pinch of sea salt
1 stick celery, chopped
1 leek, sliced
2 bay leaves
1 tablespoon fresh dill or 1 teaspoon dried dill
2 teaspoons soy sauce

Place in a large pan, bring to the boil and simmer uncovered for 1½ hours until the chickpeas are very tender and the liquid has reduced by half.

1 tablespoon extra-virgin olive oil
2 garlic cloves, crushed

Heat the oil in a pan and gently fry the garlic for 2–3 minutes until golden.

400g (14oz) can whole chestnuts
½ teaspoon paprika

Add to the garlic. Mash together and cook gently for 5 minutes. Remove bay leaves and dill from the chickpeas, add the chestnut mixture and stir well. This soup may be served as it is or liquidised for a creamy texture.

BUTTERBEAN, SWEET PEPPER AND CORIANDER SOUP

Butterbeans need to be cooked in an uncovered pot to let gas escape from them. They contain lots of trace minerals and minerals like potassium, magnesium and zinc, which are beneficial for the muscular system.
Serves 2

Preheat oven to 190°C/375°F/gas mark 5.

½ red pepper, cored and seeded, cut lengthways

Place cut-side down on a baking tray and roast in the oven or under a grill on medium high heat. When the skin has blackened and the flesh is soft, remove from the heat and leave to cool. Peel off the skin and reserve.

1 dessertspoon extra-virgin olive oil
Pinch of Hungarian paprika
1 small onion, finely chopped

Place in a large saucepan and gently fry for 10 minutes until the onion is very soft. Add the roasted red pepper and continue to gently fry for another 3–4 minutes.

400g (14oz) can butter beans, drained and rinsed
1 tablespoon finely chopped coriander
750ml (1¼ pints) water

Add to the pan. Bring to the boil, and gently simmer for 10 minutes.

Pinch of black pepper
Pinch of sea salt
2 coriander leaves, to garnish

Season, then blend in a liquidiser or food processor until smooth. Serve garnished.

BEETROOT AND ORANGE SOUP

This soup combines the nutritional and immune-stimulating properties of orange with the blood-cleansing effects of beetroot. Recent studies have shown specific anti-carcinogenic substances in beetroot – so this is more than a soup, it's also a powerful tonic. Serves 2

1 teaspoon extra-virgin olive oil **1 small onion, finely chopped**	Fry gently in a large pan, covered, for 10 minutes, until the onion is soft.
250g (9oz) raw beetroot, peeled and cut into 2.5cm (1in) dice **1 small potato, peeled and diced**	Add to the pan, cover, and sweat gently for another 5 minutes.
750ml (1¼ pints) vegetable stock	Add and bring to the boil. Simmer, covered, for 25–30 minutes until the the vegetables are soft.
Zest of ½ orange **Juice of 1 orange**	Add to the pan and simmer for 2–3 minutes. Remove from the heat and leave to cool for a few minutes.
	Blend the soup in a liquidiser or food processor until smooth. It may be difficult to get the beetroot really smooth, but don't worry – it adds a little texture.
Pinch of sea salt **Freshly ground black pepper**	Season to taste, return to the pan and reheat to serve.

neutral foods

RAW GREEN PURITY

Chlorophyll is the pigment that makes all plants the colour green. It is an effective detoxifier because it protects against toxic chemicals and inhibits the growth of germs and bacteria. Like chlorophyll, alfalfa helps guard against disease. It is a therapeutic food that contains all the known vitamins and minerals necessary for life. Alfalfa detoxifies the liver by neutralising harmful acids, thereby purifying the blood and aiding digestion. It combines with the other ingredients to make a salad that has an antioxidant, anti-inflammatory effect. It is extremely rich in amino acids, organic acids, minerals and trace minerals.

alfalfa sprouts
beetroot
cabbage
carrot
Chinese leaf
kohlrabi
green beans
turnip
grape
(a very small amount of onion or leek can be used for flavour)

There are no strict measurements as the idea is that you can make a very quick and simple salad using whatever you have available in your food store, and that the quantities can be varied to give a different taste each time you make it.

This is the essence of detox, and this recipe should become a staple, being eaten as a snack and/or with meals.

It is best made using a hand mincer, but a processor will do. Wash the vegetables and roughly chop them. Put them in the processor and blend until everything is chopped very finely. Turn into a bowl and serve. You can squeeze some fresh lemon juice over the salad to prevent browning if you wish. It will keep in the fridge for no more than a day.

SHIITAKE MUSHROOM RICE SALAD

The shiitake mushroom is a powerful stimulant for the immune system – large quantities can actually increase the body's resistance to disease. It can be used to treat a whole range of symptoms including high cholesterol levels, hypertension and colds. Serves 2

125g (4½ oz) brown rice **¼ teaspoon saffron**	Place in a pan with enough water to cover and boil for 30 minutes or until tender. Drain and leave to cool, then transfer to a salad bowl.
1 sheet nori seaweed	Toast over a flame or under the grill for a few seconds until the colour changes. Tear into pieces and add to the rice.
50g (2oz) shiitake mushrooms, sliced **1 tablespoon chopped parsley**	Add to the rice.
2 teaspoons soy sauce **Juice of ½ orange**	Mix together in a small bowl.
2.5cm (1in) root ginger, grated	Gather up all the pieces in your hand and firmly squeeze the juice into the soy and orange mixture. Pour this over the salad and mix well.
	Serve with a selection of other salads.

GUJERATI CARROT SALAD

Carrots contain large amounts of vitamins, minerals and enzymes that help to lower blood pressure, prevent infection and maintain the health of almost every organ in the body. Coriander and spring onions calm digestion and detoxify the blood. Serves 2

3 carrots, peeled and grated **2 spring onions, finely sliced** **1 tablespoon chopped coriander**	Place in a bowl.
1 teaspoon black mustard seeds	Heat a dry frying pan over a medium flame, add the seeds and dry-roast them until they begin to pop. Add to the bowl.
1 dessertspoon desiccated coconut	Dry-roast in the same way, until it turns golden brown and releases its aroma. Add to the bowl.
Pinch of sea salt **Juice of 1/2 lemon (or more to taste)**	Add and mix thoroughly. Serve chilled.

PRAWN, POTATO AND BASIL SALAD

The Chinese believe that the energy creatures possess when alive can be transferred to the eater, so prawns are an excellent choice for those who suffer from lethargy and lack drive. Potatoes draw out the toxins that the over-consumption of meat produces. Serves 2

450g (1lb) new potatoes, diced	Boil until tender, drain and leave to cool.
2 tablespoons basil leaves, torn **50g (2oz) radishes, sliced** **1 spring onion, chopped**	Place in a bowl with the potatoes and mix well.

225g (8oz) peeled prawns	Gently mix in.
Juice of ½ lime **150g (5oz) plain yogurt** **Freshly ground black pepper**	Mix together and pour over salad.
A few lettuce leaves, to serve	Arrange on a plate and place the prawn salad on top.

LOBIO (KIDNEY BEAN AND WALNUT SALAD)

When using nuts, buy them fresh in their shells. Commercially shelled nuts are generally chemically treated to process them out of their shells and to preserve them. Walnuts are rich in protein and fatty acids that eliminate impurities from the intestines and nourish the nervous system. Kidney beans are a high protein food that repair and build tissue. They improve the body's metabolism and cleanse the digestive tract.

Serves 2

400g (14oz) can red kidney beans, drained and rinsed or 170g (6oz) dried beans, soaked and boiled	Place in a bowl.
1/2 stick celery, chopped	
1 tablespoon chopped spring onion	
1 tablespoon chopped coriander	
1 tablespoon diced yellow pepper	
FOR THE DRESSING	
1 garlic clove	Blend together until the mixture is a paste.
85g (3oz) shelled walnuts	
1 tablespoon wine vinegar	
4 tablespoons water	
1 1/2 tablespoons walnut or extra-virgin olive oil	Add slowly and blend until the dressing is smooth.
Pinch of sea salt	Pour the dressing over the salad and mix well.
Freshly ground black pepper	
Pinch of cayenne pepper	
1 tablespoon chopped coriander, to garnish	Garnish and serve.

ASPARAGUS, SMOKED SALMON AND DILL SALAD

The warm and bitter quality of asparagus promotes urination, which is why it is often advised for kidney problems. It also cleanses the arteries of cholesterol, soothes skin eruptions and promotes blood circulation. Oily fish is a rich source of omega-3 essential fatty acids – nutrients that improve blood cholesterol levels and reduce inflammation of the joints, skin and other body tissues. Serves 2

8 asparagus spears	Trim off the hard woody ends. Steam or boil the spears until they are just tender, then drain. Place under a medium grill until they are just beginning to brown, then leave to cool.
2–3 leaves sweet romaine lettuce	Arrange on a serving dish.
50g (2oz) smoked salmon, cut in thin strips	Build a lattice with the asparagus.
1 dessertspoon roughly chopped dill 4–5 green olives	Arrange over the lattice.
2 teaspoons lemon juice 2 teaspoons extra-virgin olive oil	Mix together and pour over the salad.
Freshly ground black pepper	Sprinkle over the salad and serve.

CHICORY, WATERCRESS AND SEVILLE ORANGE

Bitter foods such as chicory stimulate the release of enzymes that settle the stomach and have a favourable effect on digestion. Watercress helps to break down kidney and bladder stones and is good for the health of the skin. Oranges stimulate movement of the bowels, and act as an internal antiseptic agent.

Serves 2

2 heads chicory
Juice of ¹/₂ lemon

Slice the chicory, place in a salad bowl and squeeze over the lemon juice to stop it browning.

1 bunch of watercress, stalks
   removed and roughly chopped
2 Seville oranges, peeled, sliced
   and quartered
1 carrot, grated
75ml (3fl oz) apple juice
Freshly ground black pepper

Add to the bowl and toss well.

BEANSPROUTS WITH SWEET PEPPERS AND RED CABBAGE

Sweet peppers are a rich source of vitamin C. They help to improve digestion and circulation in the body. Beansprouts contain enzymes that stimulate the body's cleansing and healing processes. They flush toxins from the body and help to destroy cancer cells. Red cabbage also improves digestion, beautifies the skin and proves useful as an ulcer remedy. Serves 2

2 handfuls mixed beansprouts
¹/₂ red pepper, cored, seeded and
   cut into thin strips
¹/₂ green pepper, cored, seeded
   and cut into thin strips
¹/₄ small red cabbage, finely sliced
Juice of 1 sweet orange

Combine in a salad bowl and serve.

COUS COUS MAGHREB

Cous cous is made from durum wheat semolina. It stimulates the liver to cleanse itself of toxins. Apricots contain large amounts of antioxidants which also help to eliminate toxins from the body. Chickpeas contain high levels of iron and are a good source of unsaturated fatty acids. Serves 2

2 teaspoons extra-virgin olive oil **1 small onion, finely chopped**	Sweat in a large pan, covered, for 5 minutes, until the onion starts to soften.
1 garlic clove, crushed **1 teaspoon mixed spice** **1 teaspoon ground coriander**	Add to the pan and sweat for another 5 minutes.
1 courgette, cut in 1cm (¹/₂ in) slices **400g (14oz) can chickpeas, drained and rinsed** **400g (14oz) can chopped tomatoes** **5 dried apricots, roughly chopped**	Add to the pan and simmer for 10–15 minutes, until the apricots begin to swell up.
300ml (¹/₂ pint) vegetable stock	Add to the pan and bring to the boil.
50g (2oz) cous cous	Add to the pan and stir well. Cover and lower the heat. Cook for 4–5 minutes, until the cous cous has puffed up and is tender.

GRILLED LEMON SOLE

Lemon sole is a temperate-water white fish that provides a superior form of protein to other types of fish. It also contains minerals such as iodine that are hard to find in other foods. Basil is an aromatic, digestion-enhancing herb. It has an antiseptic effect that makes it a good treatment for nausea and dysentery.

Serves 2

Preheat the oven to 190°C/375°F/gas mark 5.

6 cherry tomatoes
50g (2oz) fennel, sliced
2 teaspoons extra-virgin olive oil

Arrange in a small ovenproof dish, then place in the centre of the oven for 15 minutes, until tender.

2 double fillets of lemon sole, 176g (6oz) each
2 sprigs of tarragon, bruised

Place the fillets on a baking tray, skin-side uppermost. Divide the tomatoes and fennel between the fillets, arranging them on the wider end. Place one sprig of tarragon on each, then carefully fold the fish over to form a roll. Secure with a cocktail stick.

Pinch of sea salt
Freshly ground black pepper

Season, then cook under a medium hot grill until the fish begins to brown, carefully turn to cook both sides.

2 wedges of lemon, to garnish
1 teaspoon chopped tarragon, to garnish

Garnish and serve with salad or steamed vegetables.

DOUBLE-BAKED SWEET POTATOES

Sweet potatoes are one of the most nutritious vegetables and are especially useful for eliminating harmful heavy metals like mercury and lead, cadmium and copper. These toxins can remain in the body for life and cause problems with the body's metabolic system unless they are removed. Serves 2

	Preheat the oven to 190°C/375°F/gas mark 5.
2 large sweet potatoes	Bake whole for 40–50 minutes until soft.
1 teaspoon extra-virgin olive oil **1 small onion, finely chopped**	Gently fry for 5 minutes.
¹/₂ teaspoon ground cumin **¹/₂ teaspoon ground coriander** **4–5 button mushrooms, chopped**	Add to the pan and fry for another 5 minutes.
Dash of soy sauce, to taste **1 teaspoon dried oregano**	Add to the pan and remove from the heat.
	Cut each sweet potato in half lengthways and gently scoop out the flesh, being careful not to tear the skin. Add the flesh to the onion mixture and mix together well, adding more soy sauce if you like.
Sesame seeds	Place the potato skins on a non-stick baking tray and fill with the onion mixture. Sprinkle with a few sesame seeds. Bake in the centre of the oven for 20 minutes then serve immediately.

CRISPY SWEETCORN FRITTERS

This recipe is a fun and easy way to enjoy the nutritious value of corn. It is rich in vitamins A, C, E and B complex vitamins. Its vitamin B3 content stimulates circulation and reduces cholesterol levels in the blood. Soya flour from soya beans is high in calcium and contains complete protein. It has very little saturated fat and is a good source of lecithin, an essential fatty acid which can reduce inflammation and aid metabolism. Serves 2

2 tablespoons soya or gram flour **1 tablespoon polenta** **4 tablespoons water**	Mix together in a bowl with a whisk.
$1/2$ teaspoon bicarbonate of soda **$1/2$ teaspoon salt** **1 teaspoon ground coriander** **$1/2$ teaspoon ground cumin**	Add to the bowl and mix well.
200g (7oz) can sweetcorn, **rinsed and drained** **1 tablespoon chopped coriander**	Add to the bowl and stir in.
1 tablespoon sunflower oil	Heat in a heavy-based frying pan. Spoon in the batter – there should be enough for 4 fritters. Fry over a medium heat for 3–4 minutes until crisp and golden brown, then turn and cook the other side. Serve with a pungent salad such as the marinated prawns (page 33).

BUTTERBEAN AND CORIANDER POTATO CAKES

Butterbeans are highly alkalising. They neutralise acidic conditions brought about by the over-consumption of meat and refined foods, making them important for the health of the liver, lungs and skin. Serves 2

550g (1lb 5oz) potatoes, diced	Boil until tender, strain and reserve.
2 teaspoons extra-virgin olive oil **1 small onion, finely chopped** **1/2 teaspoon ground black pepper** **1/2 teaspoon ground coriander**	Gently fry for 4–5 minutes until the onions are soft but not brown.
400g (14oz) can butter beans, **drained and rinsed** **1/2 teaspoon salt** **2 tablespoons chopped coriander**	Place in a bowl with the potatoes and onion and mash together. Form the mixture into cakes.
1 tablespoon extra-virgin olive oil	Heat in a heavy non-stick pan and fry the cakes in batches to avoid over-crowding the pan. Cook for 3–4 minutes on each side until crisp and golden.
FOR THE SAUCE **2 teaspoons extra-virgin olive oil** **1 small onion, finely chopped**	Fry in a pan for 4–5 minutes until soft.
1/2 400g (14oz) can chopped tomatoes **1 teaspoon dried basil** **2 teaspoons soy sauce** **Freshly ground black pepper** **1 teaspoon cider vinegar**	Add to the pan and simmer for 20 minutes, stirring occasionally until reduced to a thick consistency.
	Serve 2 cakes per portion and top with the sauce.

FRESH BEAN CASSOULET WITH GARLIC POLENTA WEDGES

Fresh beans are useful for treating the symptoms of diabetes. Polenta is a by-product of corn, which is one of the most balanced starches that helps to prevent cancer and lowers the risk of heart disease.

Serves 2

1 dessertspoon extra-virgin olive oil
1 onion, finely chopped
1 clove garlic, crushed

Sweat in a covered pan for 10–15 minutes until the onion is soft but not brown.

1 carrot, sliced
25g (1oz) fennel, roughly chopped
85g (3oz) mushrooms, sliced
3 sprigs rosemary
1 bay leaf
1 sprig thyme

Add to the pan and sweat for another 6–7 minutes, until the mushrooms release their juices.

400g (14oz) can cannellini beans, drained and rinsed **110g (4oz) broad beans** **110g (4oz) runner beans or flat beans, sliced diagonally** **300ml ($^1/_2$ pint) vegetable stock**	Add to the pan and bring to the boil. Simmer for 15–20 minutes.
1 dessertspoon soy sauce **Freshly ground black pepper** **1 heaped teaspoon cornflour or potato flour, mixed with a little cold water**	Add to the pan and simmer for about 5 minutes to thicken the sauce.

FOR THE GARLIC POLENTA WEDGES

400ml ($^2/_3$ pint) water or vegetable stock	Bring to the boil in a large pan.
90g (3oz) polenta	Add slowly, stirring continuously.
Pinch of sea salt **Freshly ground black pepper** **1 clove garlic, crushed** **$^1/_2$ teaspoon dried mixed herbs**	Add when the mixture starts to thicken. Continue to stir until the mixture resembles a smooth porridge, 4–5 minutes.

Turn the polenta into a 23cm (9in) round, non-stick baking tin, smooth the surface and leave to cool. It will solidify. Once it is cool, cut the polenta into wedges. Transfer the wedges to a large baking sheet and cook under a high grill until crisp and brown. Serve hot with the cassoulet.

TOMATOES STUFFED WITH CHESTNUTS VIETNAMESE-STYLE

This recipe combines the cooling nature of tomatoes with the warming effect of chestnuts. Tomatoes help to purify the blood and aid in digestive problems, such as indigestion and constipation, to improve appetite. Chestnuts promote reproductive capacity and protect against premature ageing. Serves 2

	Preheat the oven to 190°C/gas mark 5.
4 large tomatoes	Slice off tops with a sharp knife. Scoop out centres with a teaspoon, being careful not to cut the skin of the tomato, or it will split when baked. Reserve the tops and centres of the tomatoes and put the tomato shells to one side.
1 teaspoon extra-virgin olive oil **½ medium onion, finely chopped** **2 garlic cloves, crushed**	Fry gently for 10–15 minutes until the onion is soft and golden.
400g (14oz) can whole chestnuts, drained and rinsed	Add to onions and mash to a lumpy paste with the back of a fork. Take the pan off the heat.
1 small handful of coriander leaf, chopped **Juice and grated rind of ½ lemon** **Pinch of salt** **Freshly ground black pepper**	Add to chestnut mixture and stir well.
	Stuff the chestnut mixture carefully into the tomato shells using a teaspoon.

FOR THE SAUCE

1 teaspoon extra-virgin olive oil
¹/₂ medium onion, finely chopped
1 mild red chilli, seeded and very
   finely chopped

Fry for 10–15 minutes until onion is soft and golden.

1 large tomato, chopped

Chop and add to pan with reserved tomato flesh and tops.

Pinch of sea salt
Freshly ground black pepper

Season then simmer uncovered for 10 minutes, until the sauce is thick. Liquidise the tomato mixture in a food processor.

Pour the sauce into an ovenproof dish large enough to take the stuffed tomatoes snugly. Sit the tomatoes on top of the sauce and bake for 30 minutes, until the tops start to brown and the tomatoes are soft. Serve with rice.

SWEET PEPPER AND CASHEW NUT FLAN

Sweet peppers regulate blood pressure and improve circulation around the body. They contain large quantities of vitamins A, B and C, and are good for health in general. The high levels of zinc, magnesium, iron and folic acid in cashew nuts function as a laxative and activate the enzymes that control energy levels. Serves 4

Preheat the oven to 190°C/375°F/gas mark 5.

1 red pepper
1 yellow pepper

Roast in the preheated oven for 20–25 minutes, or until the skins begin to turn black. Remove and place in a bowl covered with clingfilm until cool. Peel off the skins and remove the cores and seeds.

1 portion oaty pastry (see page 97)

Use to line a 30cm (12in) flan tin.

1 medium onion, sliced

Spread in the pastry case with the roasted peppers and reserve.

200g (7oz) cashew nuts

Grind in a blender or food processor until they are quite fine.

250g (9oz) spinach leaf, washed
340ml (12fl oz) soya milk
1/2 teaspoon black pepper
1 teaspoon wholegrain mustard
1/2 teaspoon paprika
1/4 teaspoon grated nutmeg
1 teaspoon salt

Add and blend until the spinach is finely chopped.

200ml (7fl oz) extra-virgin olive oil
3 teaspoons cider vinegar

Slowly add the oil and then the vinegar.

Paprika

Pour the cashew mixture over the peppers and onions, sprinkle with paprika and bake in the centre of the oven for 25 minutes, until the top has slightly browned and the flan is quite firm to touch. Serve hot or cold.

CASHEW NUT CREAM

Cashew nuts are a great source of magnesium, a nutrient that aids the functions of heart tissue and also stimulates the production of calcium, which aids bone development and growth. Cashews are high in protein and omega-6 essential fatty acids that prevent heart disease and maintain healthy cells. Use in place of dairy cream. Serves 2

110g (4oz) cashew nuts
100 ml (4 fl oz) soya milk

Place in a liquidiser and blend until creamy.

1 teaspoon runny honey
100ml (4 fl oz) sunflower oil
1 teaspoon lemon juice

Add the honey then slowly pour in the oil – you will see the mixture thicken – then finally add the lemon juice to set the cream.

MANDARIN CHEESECAKE

This cheesecake contains tofu, which has four times more protein than milk and twice as much calcium. It contains nutrients that replenish the blood and strengthen the muscles and bones. Besides being extremely low in fat, tofu is also a good source of protein and minerals. Serves 2

250g (9oz) low fat, low sugar oat biscuits	Place in a food processor and process to a fine crumb.
85g (3oz) soya margarine	Melt in a pan then add to the biscuits and process briefly. Press the mixture into a 25.5cm (10in) flan ring and refrigerate for 20 minutes to set.
570g (1¼lb) silken tofu **1 teaspoon vanilla essence**	Place in a liquidiser or food processor, and blend until smooth.
2 tablespoons concentrated apple juice or rice syrup **⅛ teaspoon powdered agar agar**	Heat the liquid in a pan and add the agar agar. Bring to a gentle simmer, stirring continuously until the grainy texture of the agar agar disappears. Add to the tofu and blend together. Pour immediately over the biscuit base and spread evenly. Refrigerate for 15 minutes to set.
200g (½lb) all fruit (no sugar or sweetener) marmalade	Heat in a pan until melted and pour evenly over the cheesecake.
2 fresh mandarins, peeled and divided into segments	Arrange on top and leave until cooled and set.

SPICED BAKED BANANAS WITH HONEY AND YOGURT

Bananas help to counteract toxins in the body. They are a source of potassium – an important mineral that helps to lower cholesterol and maintain blood pressure levels. Yogurt is also beneficial for health as it provides 'friendly' bacteria that help to protect the intestinal tract. Serves 2

Preheat the oven to 200°C/400°F/gas mark 6.

2 large bananas, peeled and sliced lengthways
1 teaspoon soya margarine

Place the bananas in a very lightly greased ovenproof dish and spread the rest of the margarine on each slice.

1 tablespoon fresh orange juice
Pinch of ground cinnamon
Pinch of ground cloves
1 cardamom pod
2 teaspoons honey

Mix together and pour over the bananas. Cover with a lid or foil and bake in the oven for 20 minutes, until the bananas are soft.

2 dessertspoons plain low-fat yogurt

Serve hot with a spoonful each.

MIXED BERRY CORN MUFFINS

The berries in this recipe are high in vitamins A and C, and contain calcium, magnesium and iron. Their fibre content stimulates digestion, and eliminates waste from the body. Rice flour contains B vitamins that are beneficial for the nervous system. Makes 10 large or 15 small muffins.

Preheat the oven to 200°C/400°F/gas mark 6.

250g (9oz) rice flour	Sift into a bowl.
170 g (6oz) polenta	
1 ½ teaspoons bicarbonate of soda	
2 tablespoons soft brown sugar	
250g (9oz) fresh or frozen mixed berries, such as cranberries, blueberries, blackberries, redcurrants or blackcurrants	Add to the bowl and mix together.
1 dessert apple, cored, peeled and grated	
170g (6oz) yogurt	Mix together in a jug, pour into the bowl and stir in to make a soft batter. You may need a little extra apple juice. It should easily spoon into a non-stick fairy cake tin, putting 1 spoonful into each case. You should have enough for 10–15 muffins.
2 tablespoons lemon juice	
1 tablespoon sunflower oil	
150ml (¼ pint) unsweetened apple juice	

Bake in the centre of the oven for 15 minutes, or until golden. Leave to cool, then transfer to a wire rack. These muffins freeze well.

APPLE AND CINNAMON CAKE

Cinnamon combined with the energy of apples encourages the body's lymphatic system to work more efficiently, thereby promoting proper circulation. It has a cleansing action due to its antiseptic, aromatic and astringent qualities. Serves 2

Preheat the oven to 190°C/375°F/gas mark 5.

85g (3oz) soya margarine
1 large tablespoon rice syrup

Cream together in a large bowl.

1 large bramley apple, peeled and grated

Mix into the bowl.

170g (6oz) wholemeal flour
1 tablespoon soya flour
1 tablespoon wheatgerm
1/2 teaspoon bicarbonate of soda
2 teaspoons ground cinnamon

Sift in to the bowl and mix together well.

50g (2oz) raisins
25ml (1fl oz) soya milk
Juice of 1/2 lemon

Add to the bowl and mix until you have the consistency of a very thick batter, adding more soya milk if necessary.

Turn the mixture into a non-stick 23cm (9in) cake tin lined with greaseproof paper. Bake on the middle shelf of the oven for 30–40 minutes, or until the cake springs back to the touch.

Leave to cool then turn out onto a wire cooling rack.

ORANGE OAT CAKE

The iodine in oats makes them useful for eliminating harmful toxins from the body. This mineral helps to regulate the body's metabolism and weight. Oats help to lower blood pressure, high cholesterol and blood sugar levels. They are a rich source of vitamin B, so they protect the nervous system of people under stress.
Serves 2

Preheat the oven to 190°C/375°F/gas mark 5.

110g (4oz) wholemeal flour
1 heaped tablespoon soya flour
2 teaspoons baking powder
1 teaspoon grated nutmeg
250g (9oz) medium oatmeal, or
oats blended to a flour
50g (2oz) wheatgerm

Mix together in a large bowl.

2 large tablespoons date syrup or
rice syrup
100ml (4fl oz) soya milk
85ml (3fl oz) water
4 tablespoons sunflower oil
Zest and juice of 1½ sweet oranges
1 heaped teaspoon sugar-free
marmalade

Mix together in a large jug. Pour into the bowl, and beat together to form a fairly firm consistency.

Turn into a 23cm (9in) non-stick cake tin lined with greaseproof paper. Bake on the middle shelf of the oven for 35–40 minutes until firm and golden. Leave in the tin for 5–10 minutes then turn out on a cooling rack.

DESSERTS and DRINKS

CITRUS DREAM

The combination of vitamin C and honey provides a quick-fix cure for any symptoms of colds, flu and coughs. This juice can also be enjoyed when you are in perfect health! Serves 1

100 ml (3¹/₂ fl oz) freshly squeezed orange juice
100ml (3¹/₂ fl oz) pineapple juice
2 dessertspoons honey
8 ice cubes
Juice of ¹/₂ lemon

Place in a liquidiser, blend well and serve immediately.

CLEANSING: CARROT, CUCUMBER AND SPINACH JUICE

This juice is strongly detoxifying and is very calming for the digestion. Aloe vera is non-toxic and has powerful healing qualities that help to alleviate ulcers and gastro-intestinal disease. It is also reputed to have anti-cancer properties. Wild blue-green algae has been described as a 'superfood' because of its great harmonising effects on body and mind. It contains practically every known nutrient; it builds the blood, acts as a liver stimulant and can relieve depression. Serves 1

4 carrots
quarter of a large cucumber
1 small handful fresh spinach leaves

Wash the vegetables well, and push them through a juicing machine (be careful not to use too much spinach as the flavour can be very strong).

$^{1}/_{2}$ teaspoon aloe vera
$^{1}/_{2}$ teaspoon wild blue-green algae

Add the aloe vera and blue green algae supplements, stir very well and serve.

PURITY: BEETROOT, CELERY, APPLE AND CARROT JUICE

This classic blend of vegetables and apple contains beta-carotene, which helps to cleanse the skin. It works by stimulating the growth and regeneration of skin cells while helping to protect against the development of cancer cells. The juice has other benefits, too. If you suffer from digestive problems, you will find this a soothing remedy. It also lowers high blood pressure and calms rheumatic pains. Serves 1

$^{1}/_{2}$ large beetroot, raw
2 sticks celery
2 apples
4 carrots

Push through a juicing machine and serve in a chilled glass.

BARLEY WATER

Barley water is a very alkalising and efficient blood cleanser that is effective in the treatment of cystitis. It can help build the stomach and spleen, making it useful for indigestion and general stomach pain. Drink this juice for an energy boost, as it is also a fatigue-reliever. Serves 1

Take 1 cup of whole barley and soak overnight in water. If you can't manage to soak the barley overnight, soak it for at least an hour before boiling the grain. Cook the grain in 3 cups of water until the grain is soft. Discard the grain and strain the water into a container, then leave to cool. Add lemon juice and honey to taste (avoid honey if there are symptoms of candidasis present). Store in the refrigerator for up to a week. Drink half a glass every morning, preferably on an empty stomach.

FLAT BREAD

This bread is an excellent way of enjoying grains and is an ideal accompaniment to any meal. It is preferable to eat complex carbohydrates with other grains and legumes, rather than with animal meat. Makes 6

60g (2¹/₂ oz) wholemeal flour
60g (2¹/₂ oz) plain white flour

Place in a bowl.

75–100ml (3–4fl oz) water

Add very slowly until you can form a soft dough (if you add too much, simply flour your hands and mix until a soft dough forms). Knead the dough for 5–6 minutes, shape into a ball, cover with a damp cloth and leave for 20 minutes.

Form the dough into 6 small balls and keep covered with the damp cloth. Heat a heavy-based frying pan over a medium low heat without oil, this will take a few minutes.

Optional:
1 teaspoon sesame seeds
1 teaspoon black mustard seeds

Take a ball and flatten it onto a lightly floured surface. Dust with flour, and sesame or mustard seeds, if desired, and roll it out thinly and evenly into a 13–15cm (5–6in) round. Place in the hot pan and cook for 1–2 minutes, until bubbles begin to form. Turn over and cook the other side for 30–60 seconds. Keep warm on a plate covered by a tea towel. Repeat with the other balls and serve immediately.

CARAWAY RYE BREAD

Rye has a very low calorific value, which makes it popular with people watching their weight. Caraway encourages digestion of the nutrients in rye. It also strengthens and tones the stomach. This bread freezes well. Makes 2 small loaves.

Preheat oven to 200°C/400°F/gas mark 6.

450g (1lb) rye flour
300g (11oz) rice flour
1 teaspoon salt

Sift into a large bowl.

15g (½oz) instant dried yeast

Mix into the bowl.

300ml (½ pint) apple juice
300ml (½ pint) hot water

2 tablespoons honey
1 tablespoon caraway seeds

Mix until liquid is at blood heat. Make a well in the flour, add the liquid and stir into the flour.

Water

Add and mix until it forms a dough. Transfer to a floured surface and knead well for 10 minutes. Divide into 2 equal portions and place in 2 small non-stick loaf tins, or shape into loaves and place on a non-stick baking sheet. Gently cover with clean tea towels and leave in a warm place until the loaves have doubled in size.

Caraway seeds

Sprinkle over the tops of the loaves. Bake in the centre of the oven for 45 minutes or until risen and the loaves sound hollow when knocked on the bottom. Leave to cool for a little before turning onto wire cooling racks.

MALTED SUNFLOWER OAT BREAD

Sunflower seeds are said to be a perfect food. They tonify the chi, which means they provide a lot of energy for the body. They contain high levels of polyunsaturated fatty acids and help to remove toxins from the body. Oats help to soothe and restore the nervous and reproductive systems and are low in fat. Makes 2 small loaves

Preheat the oven to 180°C/350°F/gas mark 4.

500g (1lb 2oz) porridge oats

Place in a food processor and blend to a fine flour.

6g (¹/₄oz) instant dried yeast
2 tablespoons sunflower seeds
1 teaspoon salt

Place in a large bowl with the oat flour.

2 tablespoons malt extract
400ml (²/₃ pint) warm water
1 tablespoon sunflower oil

Mix together, make a well in the flour and pour in the liquid. Mix together and then form into a dough.

Knead the dough for 10 minutes until it is elastic, then divide into 2 portions and place in 2 small non-stick loaf tins. Cover with a clean cloth and leave in a warm place for 30 minutes until the dough has slightly.

Bake in the centre of the oven for 50–60 minutes until the bread is browned and risen, and it sounds hollow when tapped on the bottom. Turn out onto a wire rack until cooled.

SIMPLE SODA BREAD

This is a yeast-free bread that is ideal for people with candidasis – the overgrowth of candida (yeast-like fungi) in the body. Makes 1 large loaf

Preheat the oven to 200°C/400°F/gas mark 6.

450g (1lb) wholemeal flour
225g (8oz) strong white bread flour
1½ teaspoons bicarbonate of soda
1 level dessertspoon baking powder
Pinch of sea salt

Mix together in a large bowl.

450g (1lb) low-fat plain yogurt
mixed with 150ml (¼ pint) water
1 teaspoon runny honey

Make a well in the centre and pour in gradually. Stir to mix, and then knead gently to form a dough, soft and moist, but not sticky. Do not knead too much, just enough to form an even dough.

Shape the dough into a round loaf on a greased baking sheet, and score a cross in the top. Bake in the centre of the oven for 40–50 minutes, until browned, or until it sounds hollow when tapped on the bottom. Leave to cool on a wire rack covered with a clean cloth.

For best taste and texture eat while still warm.

VEGAN PANCAKES

Vegan diets do not contain any animal products, including eggs and dairy produce – the two most common allergies in people's diets. This recipe for pancakes is a very healthy alternative. Makes 4 pancakes

50g (2oz) self-raising flour **Pinch of sea salt** **Pinch of ground black pepper**	Place in a bowl.
150ml (¼ pint) soya milk	Add slowly, mixing with a whisk to form a smooth batter.
2 tablespoons sunflower oil	Add to the batter and whisk thoroughly.
1 teaspoon lemon juice	Add to the batter and mix well. Leave to stand for about 10 minutes before cooking.

HOW TO SPROUT BEANS

You can grow sprouts from several different types of bean, but they should be grown separately as they grow at different rates. Try sprouting mung beans, soya beans, brown or green lentils, aduki beans, chickpeas and alfalfa seeds. The method is the same for them all.

Start a new jar every couple of days so that you have a continual supply. The sprouts will also grow quite well on a kitchen surface, where it's less easy to forget to rinse them, but they will not grow so big.

1 wide-necked jar

Beans or lentils to fill $\frac{1}{3}$ of the jar, soaked overnight, then drained and well rinsed	Place in the jar.
Piece of fine-mesh material (eg. new dishcloth) **Elastic band**	Cover the opening with the material and secure with the elastic band.
	Lay the jar on its side and leave in a warm dark place. Rinse the sprouts with lukewarm water at least 3 times a day. Try not to disturb the sprouts too much, as they may break. Drain off the water as thoroughly as you can (you don't need to remove the material).
	After 3–4 days your sprouts will be ready to eat. They will keep in the fridge in plastic bags for a few days.

BREAKFAST MUESLI

Oats are full of protein, vitamins and minerals, making them an excellent energy-giving food. Their body-building properties lower blood sugar levels, nourish bones and teeth, and are vital for a healthy nervous system.

5 parts rice flakes
2 part wheatgerm
5 parts oats
1 part flaked almonds
1 part chopped hazelnuts
1 part sunflower seeds
1 part sesame seeds
1 part pumpkin seeds
1 part dried apricots, chopped
1 part dried figs, chopped
1 part raisins

You can make up as much muesli in advance as you wish, and keep it in an airtight container.

raspberries
plums
soya milk

Serve with soya milk, topped with the fresh fruit. Soak the muesli in the soya milk for 10–20 minutes before serving.

OATY PASTRY

Complete carbohydrates such as oats are perhaps the most efficient of foods in the Western diet. Use this oaty pastry wherever recipes call for savoury shortcrust pastry. The nutritional and healing properties of oats range from reducing cholesterol levels to strengthening the spleen and pancreas. They can be used where there is nervous weakness or a digestive problem. Makes 1 portion

250g (9oz) wholemeal flour
100g (4oz) oats
25g (1oz) ground almonds
25g (1oz) sesame seeds
¹/₂ teaspoon dried thyme

Place in a large bowl.

1 teaspoon soy sauce
2¹/₂ tablespoons extra-virgin olive oil

Add to the bowl and rub together lightly with the fingertips until the mixture resembles fine breadcrumbs.

Gradually mix in cold water a little at a time until the pastry binds together but is not too wet. Leave to stand for 10 minutes.

Roll out the pastry on a lightly floured surface. When it becomes difficult to roll, transfer it to a 30cm (12in) non-stick flan ring and push it into shape with your fingers.

Bake on the middle shelf of the oven for 10 minutes, then remove from the oven and leave to cool.

cooling foods

cooling foods

for hot people

Hot people feel hot, dislike heat or are attracted to the cold. Too much heat in the body can be due to a number of factors such as:

- **eating too many warming foods (see page 8) and/or not enough cooling foods**
- **working very hard or being over-active**
- **over-consumption of alcohol, coffee, cigarettes and synthetic drugs**
- **emotional stress**
- **fatigue**
- **exposure to an extremely hot climate**
- **an obstruction to an internal organ**

If you are a hot person, avoid foods that will heat you up even more. Stimulants such as coffee, alcohol and sugar and the overuse of heating spices, such as chilli and pepper, should be avoided by a hot person. When cooling foods are eaten, the energy and fluids of the body are directed inwards and downwards so that the upper parts of the body cool down first. Hot people can eat some of the foods with neutral energy because they will not add further warmth to their bodies.

Some cooking techniques, like pressure-cooking, baking and deep-frying can turn a cooling food into a warming food. Instead of using these methods, hot people should steam or simmer foods and eat raw foods, which are more cooling than cooked food.

CALDO VERDE

Potato and cabbage are very detoxifying vegetables. Potatoes are mildly diuretic and help to neutralise body acids – great news for sufferers of arthritis and rheumatism. Cabbage is one of the best cures for many digestive problems, such as constipation and bloating. It contains compounds that studies have shown inhibit cancerous growths in the gastro-intestinal tract. Serves 2

900ml (1½ pints) vegetable stock	Bring to the boil in a pan.
1 small onion, finely chopped **2 medium potatoes, sliced**	Add to the pan and simmer for 15 minutes.
2–3 dark green cabbage leaves, **cut in 1 x 3cm (½ x 1¼ in) slices**	Add to the pan and simmer for another 15 minutes, until the vegetables are cooked.
1 tablespoon chopped oregano **1 dessertspoon fresh lemon juice** **Dash of soy sauce**	Add to the pan and simmer for 5 more minutes. This soup is best served unblended but you may want to liquidise it for a smooth consistency.

SOUPS

GOLDEN PEARL BARLEY SOUP

Barley is a good source of B-complex vitamins, iron, calcium, phosphorous and potassium. It is a great nourishing and strengthening grain with a strong diuretic effect. The high water content of beansprouts makes them useful for flushing out toxins from the body. They also contain vitamin E, which promotes proper blood circulation. Serves 2

250ml (9fl oz) vegetable stock	Heat in a pan.
1 onion, finely chopped **1 stick celery, finely chopped**	Add to the pan and simmer for 5 minutes.
40g (1½ oz) pearl barley **Pinch of saffron** **Pinch of mixed herbs**	Add to the pan and simmer for 30 minutes.
50g (2oz) swede, diced **1 carrot, chopped** **350ml (12fl oz) vegetable stock**	Add to the pan, cover and simmer for another 20 minutes, until the barley and vegetables are tender.
Dash of soy sauce **Ground black pepper** **Handful of mung beansprouts**	Add to the pan, simmer for 2–3 minutes and serve.

CREAMY MUSHROOM SOUP

Mushrooms help to neutralise the toxins created by our consumption of meat. They are also a rich source of germanium, which increases resistance to disease. Soya milk is the primary source of lecithin, a nutrient that helps to control and lower cholesterol. Celery has a high water content, which means it has few calories and is very alkalising. Serves 2

1 small onion, sliced **1 small stick celery, finely chopped** **1 tablespoon vegetable stock**	Place in a large pan and gently sweat, covered, for 10 minutes, until the onion is softened.
125g (4¹/₂ oz) button mushrooms, **thinly sliced** **2 tablespoons vegetable stock** **¹/₂ teaspoon dried sage**	Add to the pan and stir. Cover and sweat for another 10 minutes.
1 tablespoon soy sauce **500ml (18fl oz) vegetable stock**	Add to the pan and bring to the boil. Simmer for 15 minutes.
1 heaped teaspoon cornflour **blended with a little cold water**	Remove the pan from the heat and leave to cool for 2–3 minutes. Stir in the cornflour mixture, then return to a very low heat to thicken.
2 tablespoons soya milk **Soy sauce, optional**	Add to the pan and simmer very gently for 2 minutes, stirring occasionally. Check the seasoning – you may wish to add some more soy sauce. This soup can be blended for a smoother texture.

SWEETCORN CHOWDER

Sweetcorn is packed with nutrients and enzymes, such as vitamin B3. The 'extra' virgin status of olive oil means that it has less acidity than normal virgin oil and so is better quality. It also has a distinctive aromatic flavour. Serves 2

1 teaspoon extra-virgin olive oil
1 small onion, finely chopped
1 small stick celery, finely chopped

Place in a large pan, covered, and sweat gently for 6–7 minutes, until the onion is softened.

$1/2$ teaspoon ground coriander
$1/2$ courgette, sliced
2 fresh tomatoes, finely chopped

Add to the pan, cover, and sweat for 5 minutes.

400g (14oz) can sweetcorn, drained and well rinsed
750ml (1$1/4$ pints) vegetable stock
2 teaspoons soy sauce

Add to the pan and bring to the boil, then simmer for 20 minutes.

1 small handful of coriander, chopped
Extra soy sauce, to taste
Pinch of freshly ground black pepper

Add to the pan and simmer for another 2–3 minutes, then remove from the heat.

Leave to cool for a few minutes, then blend to a creamy texture in a liquidiser or food processor. Return to the pan to reheat.

Coriander leaves, to garnish

Serve garnished.

CHILLED ASPARAGUS AND LEMON SOUP

Chinese nutritionists believe that asparagus 'tonifies the yin'. This means that it lubricates dryness in the body, making it good for conditions like diabetes. Lemons stimulate the liver and gall bladder to eliminate toxins. The acidity in them destroys the harmful bacteria that causes bloating, flatulence and indigestion.

Serves 2

275g (10oz) asparagus, trimmed and peeled	Cut off the tips and reserve. Cut into thin strips 2–3cm ($^3/_4$–1$^1/_4$in) long.
100ml (4fl oz) water	Heat in a pan.
1 small onion, finely chopped	Add to the pan, cover and simmer gently for 5 minutes.
1 medium potato, peeled and diced **800ml (1$^1/_3$ pints) water** **Salt and freshly ground black pepper**	Add to the pan with the asparagus strips and simmer for 10 minutes, until the potato and asparagus are very soft.
2 tablespoons chopped oregano **Juice of 1 lemon**	Add to the pan and simmer for 2–3 minutes, then blend in a liquidiser or food processor.
	Steam the asparagus tips for 2–3 minutes until just tender and add to the smooth soup.
Lemon zest, to garnish	Chill and serve garnished.

cooling foods

TOMATO, APPLE AND CELERY SOUP

All the ingredients in this cleansing soup are alkalising once digested. This means they are helpful in treating stress, which causes an acidic build up in the body. Serves 2

1 teaspoon extra-virgin olive oil **2 sticks celery, chopped** **1 small onion, finely chopped**	Place in a large pan, covered, and sweat for 10 minutes, until the onion is softened.
8 fresh tomatoes, puréed **1 dessert apple, peeled, cored and diced** **1 teaspoon dried marjoram**	Add to the pan, bring to the boil and simmer gently for 10 minutes.
600ml (1 pint) vegetable stock	Add to the pan, bring back to the boil and simmer for 10 minutes.
Soy sauce, to serve	Serve immediately.

CLEANSING WATERCRESS SOUP

Watercress is an excellent cooling nourishing tonic for mind and body. It is also a blood cleanser and is especially good when you feel stressed and run down. Egyptian pharaohs gave watercress juice to their slaves twice a day, as they believed it would increase their productivity. Serves 2

250ml (9fl oz) vegetable stock	Heat in a large pan.
3–4 spring onions, finely chopped **Pinch of ground nutmeg** **¹/₂ teaspoon dried thyme** **1 bay leaf**	Add to the pan, cover and simmer for 5 minutes.
1 medium potato, peeled and sliced **450ml (³/₄ pint) vegetable stock**	Add to the pan, cover and simmer for a further 20 minutes, until the potato is cooked.
2 bunches of watercress, washed and roughly chopped **Pinch of sea salt**	Add to the pan and simmer for 2 minutes.
200ml (7fl oz) soya milk	Turn off the heat and add. Stir well and leave to stand for 5 minutes.
Freshly ground black pepper **Sprig of watercress, to garnish**	Blend in a food processor or liquidiser until smooth and creamy. Reheat in a pan, season and serve garnished.

RAW YIN PURITY

The cooling properties in these ingredients are exceedingly healing. They have a moistening effect on the organs, so are useful for protection against inflammation, gastritis, hepatitis and swollen glands. Cooling foods have therapeutic effects on headaches and depression, which can often be linked to an overheated liver that has begun to perform its cleansing and disease-fighting functions less efficiently.

apple
celery
chicory
pear
marjoram
broccoli
radish
Swiss chard
mungbean sprouts
spinach
cauliflower
(a very small amount of chive can
   be used for flavour)

There are no measurements as the idea is that you can make a very quick and simple salad using whatever you have available in your food store, and that the quantities can be varied to give a different taste each time you make it.

This is the essence of detox, and this recipe should become a staple, being eaten as a snack and/or with meals.

It is best made using a hand mincer, but a processor will do. Wash the vegetables and roughly chop them. Put them in the processor and blend until everything is chopped very finely. Turn into a bowl and serve.

You can squeeze some fresh lemon juice over the salad to prevent browning if you wish. It will keep in the fridge for no more than a day.

AVOCADO AND STRAWBERRY SALAD

Food combining enables the proper digestion of different food groups. Fats and oils such as those found in avocado combine perfectly with the acidity of strawberries. When digested, they breakdown at a similar rate, allowing complete absorption of their nutrients into the body. Serves 2

1 ripe avocado, halved, stoned, peeled and cut into cubes **6 strawberries, hulled and quartered**	Place in a bowl.
2 teaspoons lemon juice **2 teaspoons balsamic vinegar**	Pour over and mix together gently.
Freshly ground black pepper	Season and serve.

AVOCADO, CHERRY TOMATO AND SPINACH SALAD

All the ingredients in this salad improve vitality, due to the rich source of fats, protein, vitamin A, beta-carotene and chlorophyll that they provide. Limes have an antiseptic quality and this, combined with the laxative actions of honey, help to purify the blood. Serves 2

1 ripe avocado, halved, stoned, peeled and cubed	Place in a salad bowl.
8 cherry tomatoes, halved	
1 handful of baby spinach, washed, dried and torn into pieces	
Juice of 1 lime	Combine in a jug and pour over the salad. Mix gently and serve.
1 teaspoon honey	
Pinch of sea salt	

SOYA MAYONNAISE

Soya is said to decrease cholesterol and prevent breast and ovarian cancers due to its phytoestrogen activity. Phytoestrogens are plant oestrogens that have a positive effect on the menopause and are generally helpful in ensuring reproductive health. Serves 2

250ml (9fl oz) soya milk	Place in a food processor and blend.
$1/2$ teaspoon sea salt	
$1/2$ teaspoon black pepper	
$1/2$ teaspoon paprika	
1 teaspoon dried basil	
$1/4$ teaspoon wholegrain mustard	
1 teaspoon honey	

150ml ($\frac{1}{4}$ pint) extra-virgin olive oil	Set the food processor to high speed and pour in the oil gradually. You will see the milk begin to emulsify.
2 teaspoons cider or white wine vinegar	Add and blend. This will give the mayonnaise a thicker consistency.

SNOWDRIFT SALAD

Cauliflower cleanses the blood of impurities and toxins and can also be beneficial for high blood pressure. Studies have shown that cauliflower has anti-cancerous and antioxidant compounds that protect against breast and colon cancer. This is a very light salad and can be served to accompany a main dish, or other, more substantial, salads. Serves 2

1 small or $\frac{1}{2}$ large cauliflower, divided into small florets	Place in a liquidiser or food processor and blend until the cauliflower resembles cous cous. Transfer to a salad bowl.
10–15 white seedless grapes, cut in half **2.5cm (1in) cucumber, finely diced** **Juice of $\frac{1}{2}$ lemon, to taste** **Pinch of sea salt, optional**	Add to the bowl and toss gently.

HERBY POLENTA CRACKERS

Polenta is cooked cornmeal. It is one of the most balanced starches and is very easy to digest. It has a diuretic effect, thereby helping the kidneys to excrete waste products and regulating proper digestion.

Makes 8 crackers

Preheat the oven to 180°C/350°F/gas mark 4.

310ml (11fl oz) boiling water

Bring to the boil in a small, tall-sided pan.

110g (4oz) medium polenta
1 teaspoon mixed dried herbs

Add slowly, stirring continuously until you have the consistency of a smooth porridge.

¹/₂ teaspoon sea salt
25g (1oz) soya margarine

Remove the pan from the heat and add, mixing thoroughly. You may need to add a little extra water if the mixture is too stiff.

Spoon the batter onto very lightly greased non-stick baking sheets, spreading each spoonful into an even circle, then score each circle into triangles.

Bake in the oven for 20 minutes, or until the crackers are golden brown and crispy. Leave to cool on wire racks. Serve with dips and soups.

AUBERGINE AND CORIANDER DIP

Especially good for those who experience strong heat symptoms, this cooling snack cleanses the blood and protects against arterial damage made by the build-up of cholesterol. Serves 2

Preheat the oven to 190°C/375°F/ gas mark 5.

1 large aubergine

Bake whole with the stalk left on for 40 minutes, or until the skin has browned and it feels very soft to touch. Leave to cool, then peel.

1 garlic clove, crushed
½ teaspoon sea salt
¼ teaspoon ground black pepper
¼ teaspoon ground cumin
2 dessertspoons extra-virgin olive oil

Place in a liquidiser or food processor along with the aubergine flesh, and blend until smooth.

1 tablespoon chopped coriander

Stir into the mixture and serve with flat bread (see page 90).

BLACKENED SAVOY, MANGETOUT AND BABY CORN WITH SESAME SEEDS AND LEMON

Vegetables are high in calcium and sesame is a good source of both calcium and protein, making this dish ideal for strengthening bones, teeth and blood. Legumes contain almost as much protein as animal products, so this recipe is ideal for people who don't eat dairy foods. Serves 2

2 teaspoons sesame or extra-virgin olive oil	Using kitchen paper, wipe a wok or large frying pan with a thin coating of the oil, then heat over a high heat for a few seconds.
2 large savoy cabbage leaves, cut into 1 x 4cm (¹/₂ x 1¹/₂ in) strips **12–14 mangetout** **6–8 whole baby corn, cut in half lengthways**	Add to the pan and stir-fry until the vegetables begin to get blackened, 2–3 minutes.
1 teaspoon sesame seeds	Add to the pan and stir-fry for 30 seconds.
2–3 dashes soy sauce **2 teaspoons lemon juice**	Stir into the pan then cover for 1 minute to steam the vegetables. Serve hot or warm.

JAPANESE SPRING SALAD

Soya beans are unique among legumes, in that they contain all eight essential amino acids, making them a perfectly balanced protein food. This dish will help to lower cholesterol and is also useful for post-menopausal women because of its plant oestrogen content. Serves 2

85g (3oz) dried soya beans, soaked overnight, or 125g (4½oz) canned beans

Cook the drained beans in water until soft, for about 1 hour, then drain and leave to cool. If using canned beans, drain and rinse well. Place in a salad bowl.

100g (3½oz) baby spinach leaf
25g (1oz) rocket

Tear into pieces, removing tough stalks, and add to the beans.

125g (4½oz) radishes, finely sliced
50g (2oz) mangetout, sliced diagonally
1 mandarin orange, peeled and segmented

Add to the beans.

FOR THE DRESSING
100g (3½oz) silken tofu
2 tablespoons orange juice
2 tablespoons soy sauce
1 dessertspoon wholegrain mustard
1 dessertspoon cider vinegar
Pinch of sea salt
Freshly ground black pepper

Place all the ingredients in a liquidiser or food processor and blend until smooth and creamy. Pour over the salad and gently mix together.

MIXED WHOLEGRAIN SALAD, WITH MISO AND TARRAGON DRESSING

Wholegrains should make up about 40 per cent of our diet. Barley, groats and millet protect against cancer and heart disease, while nourishing and soothing the digestive tract and liver. Miso is a fermented soya bean paste that is high in protein and B12, a vitamin found mostly in meat and milk, making this salad an ideal choice for vegans. Serves 2

50g (2oz) whole wheatberries, soaked for 12 hours and drained **50g (2oz) pot barley**	Bring a large pan of water to the boil and put in the grains. Bring back to the boil and simmer for 50–60 minutes, until the grains are tender. Drain well and place in a bowl.
50g (2oz) buckwheat groats	Dry-roast in a pan over a medium heat, until they give off a nutty aroma. Add plenty of water to cover, bring to the boil and simmer for 10–15 minutes until tender. Drain well and add to the other grains.
FOR THE DRESSING **2 teaspoons brown miso** **2 teaspoons cider vinegar** **2 teaspoons soy sauce** **1 teaspoon extra-virgin olive oil**	Mix together and stir into the hot grains. As the grains cool down they will absorb the dressing.

1 dessertspoon sesame seeds,
  toasted

1 small carrot, peeled and grated

1–2 dessertspoons raisins

1 tablespoon finely diced cucumber

1 small handful fresh tarragon, tough
  stalks removed and roughly chopped

Place in a bowl and add to the grains once they are completely cool. Mix well and serve. You can add more miso for a stronger flavour.

CHICKPEA, POTATO AND SPINACH SALAD WITH MINT YOGURT DRESSING

Chickpeas and potatoes are beneficial for the body as a whole, because of the high content of nutrients such calcium, potassium, beta-carotene, folic acid and vitamin C. In Chinese medicine, the subtle, bland flavour of potato is believed to have a very calming effect on the digestive process. This makes it a tonic for digestive problems. Both potatoes and chickpeas neutralise acid and soothe inflammation in the body.

Serves 2

225g (8oz) cooked chickpeas

2 medium potatoes, cooked and diced

1 small handful fresh spinach,
  stalks removed, torn

Place in a bowl.

FOR THE DRESSING

1½ tablespoons plain yogurt

1 teaspoon tamarind juice

1 teaspoon honey

1 teaspoon finely chopped mint

Mix thoroughly until smooth and pour over the potato salad. Toss well.

1–2 mint leaves

Serve garnished.

MONGO – FILIPPINO MUNG BEANS WITH SPINACH AND TOMATO

This recipe is rich in iron, vitamins and chlorophyll, which all have a very cooling and calming influence on the body and mind. Serves 2

85g (3oz) dried mung beans, rinsed **500ml (18fl oz) water** **1 bay leaf**	Place in a pan and bring to the boil. Boil for 2 minutes then turn down the heat and simmer for 1–1¹/₂ hours until the beans are tender and almost mushy.
1 tablespoon extra-virgin olive oil **1 garlic clove, crushed** **1 small onion, finely chopped**	Fry gently in a frying pan until the onion is soft and golden.
170g (6oz) tomatoes, peeled and chopped	Add and fry gently until all the excess liquid is gone. Add to the mung beans and simmer for 5 minutes, stirring occasionally.
125g (4¹/₂oz) spinach, washed, drained and coarsely chopped **1 dessertspoon lime juice** **Pinch of sea salt**	Add to the beans and simmer until the spinach is cooked, about 5 minutes.
2 wedges of lime, to garnish	Serve with rice or millet, garnished.

cooling foods

CORN ENCHILADAS FILLED WITH TOFU, SPINACH AND SALSA

Tofu contains lots of B12, an essential vitamin often deficient in vegetarians. Its cooling nature helps to relieve inflammation of the stomach and neutralises toxins in the body. Serves 2

Preheat the oven to 190°C/375°F/gas mark 5.

½ packet smoked tofu, sliced

Place on a non-stick baking tray and brown under a medium grill, turning once. Leave to cool and reserve.

1 teaspoon extra-virgin olive oil
2 handfuls spinach leaves, chopped
2 dessertspoons soy sauce

Using kitchen paper, wipe a wok or large frying pan with the oil. Add the spinach and soy sauce to the wok with the tofu. Stir-fry for 2–3 minutes over a medium heat, then remove from the heat and reserve.

FOR THE SALSA
6 tomatoes, skinned and chopped,
1 small onion
¼ teaspoon ground cumin
1 handful coriander leaves, chopped
Juice of ½ lime
Pinch of sea salt
Freshly ground black pepper
2 teaspoons extra-virgin olive oil

Place in a liquidiser or food processor and blend until quite finely chopped.

4 corn taco shells

Divide the spinach mixture between the taco shells and place on their sides in an ovenproof dish. Cover with the salsa and bake in the oven for about 30 minutes until heated through.

½ avocado, sliced, to garnish
Coriander leaves, to garnish

Garnish and serve hot with a side salad.

MARINATED GRILLED VEGETABLES

It is important to consume vegetables daily for their therapeutic high-fibre low-fat qualities. Marinating and grilling vegetables accentuates their full flavour and brings out their healing properties. Serves 2

cooling foods

FOR THE MARINADE
1 tablespoon extra-virgin olive oil
1 tablespoon balsamic vinegar
Freshly ground black pepper
Pinch of salt
1 teaspoon honey
2 teaspoons lemon juice

Mix and reserve.

1 aubergine, sliced into 1cm ($^1/_2$ in)
    rounds
1 red pepper, cut in half lengthways,
    cored and seeded
1 red onion, sliced lengthways
2 courgettes, sliced lengthways
    5mm ($^1/_4$ in) thick
6 cherry tomatoes
4 asparagus spears, trimmed

Place under a high grill until the vegetables begin to blacken and are soft. The red pepper should be cooked skin-side up. Remove from the heat and allow to cool. Peel off the red pepper skin and cut into strips. Place the vegetables in a bowl.

Small handful of oregano, chopped
Small handful of basil, chopped
Small handful of parsley, chopped
$^1/_2$ 400g (14oz) can kidney beans,
    drained and rinsed

Add to the bowl. Pour over the marinade and mix well. Leave to marinate for 1–2 hours.

This recipe is very good served with the flat breads (see page 90).

TOFU AND PINEAPPLE STIR-FRY

Tofu contains as much calcium as milk and is very low in calories. Pineapples have a strong diuretic action which helps the detoxification process; they also contain an enzyme that aids proper digestion. Serves 2

FOR THE SAUCE

1 small can pineapple chunks Place in a food processor or liquidiser and blend until smooth.

1 red chilli, seeded and finely chopped

1 garlic clove, crushed

2.5cm (1in) root ginger, peeled and finely grated

2 tablespoons soy sauce

2 tablespoons cider vinegar

1 teaspoon cornflour

¼ packet plain tofu, cut into cubes Grill for 5 minutes under a medium heat until golden brown.

2 teaspoons extra-virgin olive oil Heat in a wok or large frying pan until hot.

2 spring onions, sliced Add to the wok and stir-fry for 2 minutes.

¼ red pepper, seeded and sliced

½ carrot, sliced in strips

½ courgette, sliced diagonally Add and stir-fry for 2 minutes.

12 mangetout

1 handful of beansprouts Add to pan, and put in the grilled tofu. Stir-fry for 1 minute.

1 handful of sliced Chinese leaves

1 tablespoon chopped coriander Add the sauce and coriander. Cook for 3 minutes until bubbling.

SPAGHETTI WITH CLAMS

In Chinese medicine, clams are used to moisten dryness, nurture the yin and resolve damp conditions, such as thrush and bloating. This recipe is effective for fluid retention and helps to soften hard lumps in the body, such as kidney and gall stones. Serves 2

450g (1lb) fresh clams, well scrubbed **7 tablespoons water**	Put in a pan and cook until the shells open, about 3–5 minutes. Drain, reserving the water. Discard any shells that are still closed. Remove the clam meat from the shells and reserve.
1 tablespoon extra-virgin olive oil **1 garlic clove, cut in half lengthways**	Fry gently in a heavy pan for 3–4 minutes, then remove the garlic and discard.
400g (14oz) can chopped tomatoes	Add with the reserved clam stock and simmer for 20–25 minutes.
200g (7oz) spaghetti	Cook until *al dente* as instructed on the packet.
½ tablespoon chopped fresh parsley **1 dessertspoon fresh lemon juice** **Pinch of sea salt**	Add to the sauce with the clams and cook for 1 minute.
Freshly ground black pepper	Pile the spaghetti onto serving plates, season and spoon the clam sauce on top. Serve immediately.

CRAB AND ORANGE WRAPPED IN SWISS CHARD LEAVES

Crab contains calcium, phosphorous, iron, vitamins A, B1, B2 and niacin, giving it a strong detoxifying and anti-inflammatory effect on the body. Swiss chard is a beneficial aid to the digestive system. Serves 2

2 freshly cooked crabs	Remove the meat from the shells, separating the dark and white meat.
FOR THE SAUCE **Juice of ½ lemon** **Juice of ½ orange** **100ml (4fl oz) fish or vegetable stock**	Place in a food processor or liquidiser with the dark crab meat and blend to make a smooth sauce. Warm gently in a pan.
6 large Swiss chard leaves, stalks removed	Blanch one at a time in boiling water for 5–10 seconds, then immediately put them into cold water. Leave them to dry for a few moments. Handle very carefully so as not to break the leaves.
Pinch of turmeric **Pinch of cayenne** **Pinch of sea salt** **Freshly ground black pepper**	Add to the white crabmeat and mix gently.
2.5cm (1in) root ginger, peeled and grated	Gather it into your hand and squeeze the juice over the white crabmeat.
Chopped chives	Lay the leaves out flat and divide the white crabmeat between each leaf, placing it in the centre. Sprinkle a little chopped chives on each filling and carefully fold over the sides and then the ends. Steam the stuffed leaves for no more than 2 minutes. Pour the sauce over and serve with boiled rice, with a little coconut milk mixed into the boiling water.

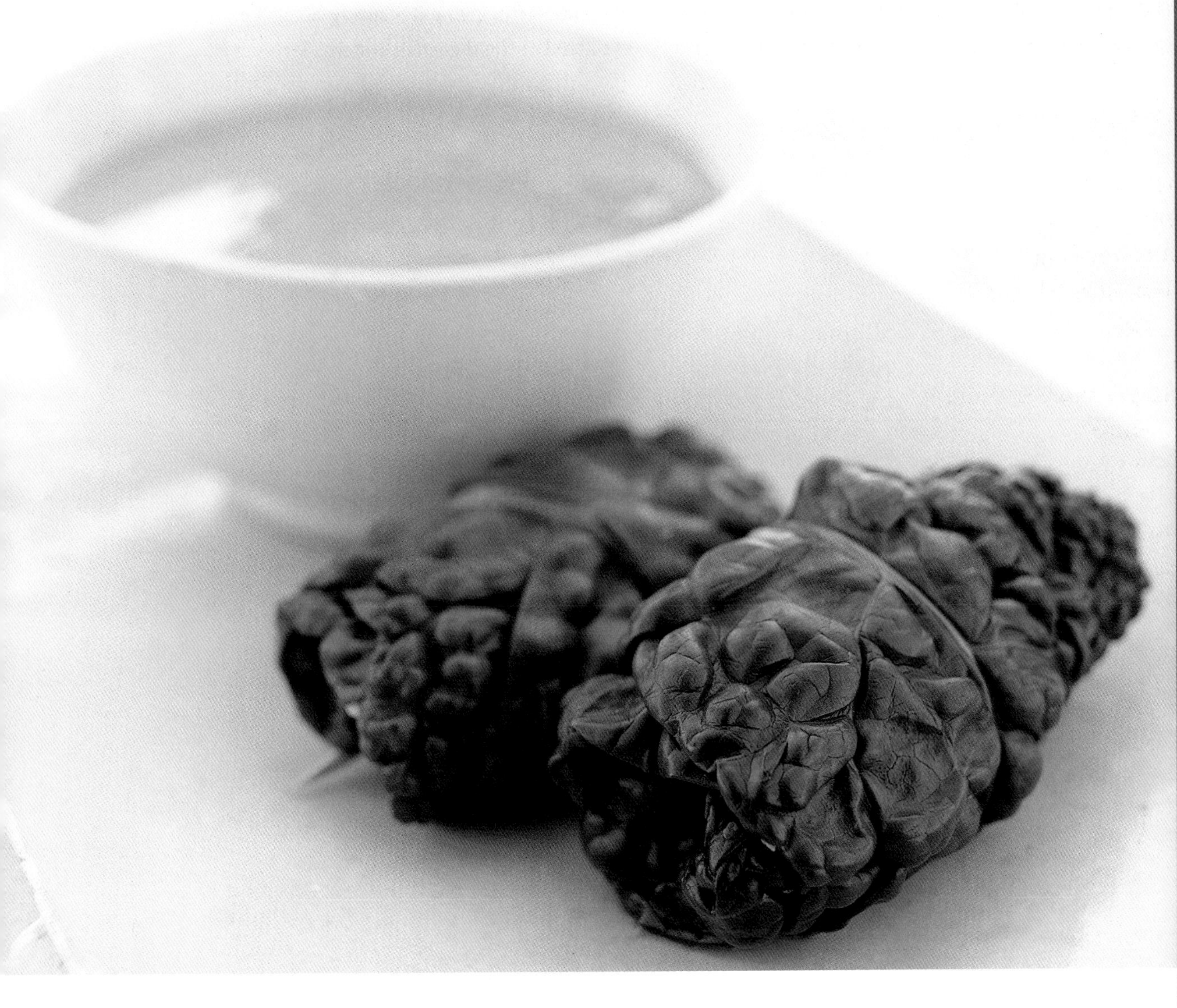

MILLET PILAFF WITH BAKED AUBERGINES

Millet – sometimes called the 'queen of the grains' – is a rich source of silicon, which helps to detoxify the body and has strong anti-fungal properties. Aubergines are rich in bioflavonoids which help to renew arteries and prevent strokes and haemorrhages. Serves 2

Preheat the oven to 180°C/350°F/gas mark 4.

FOR THE PILAFF

2 teaspoons extra-virgin olive oil **1 small onion**	Gently fry, covered, for 4–5 minutes, until the onion is softened.
1 teaspoon ground coriander **2 cloves garlic, crushed**	Add to the pan and fry for another 5 minutes.
1 dessertspoon pitted black olives **125g (4½ oz) millet**	Add to the pan and fry for another 2 minutes, until the millet starts to give off a nutty aroma.
400g (14oz) can chopped tomatoes **400ml (²/₃ pint) vegetable stock**	Add to the pan, bring to the boil and simmer for 20 minutes, uncovered. If the millet still has a slight bite you may need to add some extra water, and cook for a little longer.
1 dessertspoon flaked almonds, **toasted** **2–3 dashes soy sauce** **1 tablespoon chopped parsley**	Add when the millet is tender, then remove from the heat.

FOR THE AUBERGINES

1 medium aubergine, cut in 1cm
    (¹/₂ in) slices
1 tablespoon olive oil

Arrange the slices in an ovenproof dish and spread over the olive oil so each slice is thinly coated. Cover and bake for 10 minutes.

1 tablespoon tahini
1 tablespoon water
juice of ¹/₂ lemon
1 garlic clove, crushed
1 teaspoon soy sauce

Mix in a small bowl. Remove the aubergine slices from the oven and stir the mixture into them, coating the slices well. Return to the oven and bake uncovered for another 15 minutes or until the slices are soft and tender.

To serve, spoon the pilaff onto serving plates and top with the aubergines.

SIMPLICITY SUSHI

Salmon is low in cholesterol, has a high protein content and is easily digestible. It is a rich source of omega-3 essential fatty acids that help to maintain skin, teeth and nails. Nori, a sea vegetable, is high in protein and nutrients that help reduce cholesterol. Serves 2

225g (8oz) sushi rice or short-grain rice

Soak in cold water for 15 minutes, rinse and drain.

450ml (³/₄ pint) water

Place in a pan with the rice and bring to the boil. Stir once and cover, reduce the heat to very low and leave for 10 minutes. Turn off the heat and leave to stand, covered, for 5 minutes.

4 tablespoons rice wine vinegar or white wine vinegar
1 teaspoon caster sugar
1 teaspoon sea salt

Heat gently in a pan. Spread the rice on a large plate or tray and pour the vinegar mixture over. Stir with a fork for 5 minutes, making sure that all the rice is coated in vinegar. Leave to cool, then divide in half.

2 sheets nori seaweed

Toast quickly under a grill or over a gas flame. You will see the colour change.

85g (3oz) white crabmeat
Thin strips of cucumber
1 teaspoon sesame seeds, toasted

Place the nori sheets on 2 pieces of clingfilm. Using one half of the sushi rice, divide it between the nori sheets and spread it evenly over each sheet. Place a line of crabmeat, a few strips of cucumber and a few sesame seeds down the centre and roll up each sheet. Wrap in clingfilm and chill.

cooling foods

Make 8–10 moulds by cutting the cardboard inner tube of kitchen roll into 2.5cm (1in) sections, and lining them with foil or clingfilm.

85g (3oz) smoked salmon
Wasabi (Japanese horseradish)

Press the remaining rice into the moulds. Cut the smoked salmon into 4cm (1¹/₂in) pieces. Take a piece of smoked salmon, thinly spread a little of the wasabi paste over it and push it down on top of the rice. Chill.

TO SERVE
Dark soy sauce
Wasabi
Pickled ginger

To serve, remove the moulds. Remove the clingfilm from the sushi rolls and cut into slices. Arrange with the salmon sushi and serve.

YIN FRUIT SALAD

A raw fruit salad is an excellent way of preserving the nutrients in food. The fruits in this dish are rich in water-soluble vitamins – B complex and C – but these can be easily lost through careless storage. An excess of exposure to air, water, heat and light will rob fresh fruit of its essential goodness, so buy in season and eat when fully ripe. Serves 2

1 banana	Chop into a bowl.
¹/₂ apple	
6–8 blueberries	
¹/₂ pear	
2.5cm (1in) slice watermelon	
1 tangerine	
2–3 strawberries	
250ml (¹/₄ pint) orange and grapefruit juice mixed in equal parts	Pour over the fruit.
1 dessertspoon yogurt, to serve	Serve topped with the yogurt.

GOOSEBERRY FOOL

Gooseberries help the liver to eradicate waste products. They also contain digestive enzymes that enable the proper and complete breakdown of protein. This pudding is a therapeutic treat. Serves 2

125g (4¹/₂ oz) fresh gooseberries, topped and tailed
2 tablespoons honey or apple juice concentrate
2 tablespoons fresh orange juice

Place in a pan, bring to the boil and simmer until tender.

125g (4¹/₂ oz) plain tofu
¹/₂ teaspoon lemon juice
1 tablespoon sunflower oil

Blend in a liquidiser or food processor and then add the gooseberries. Liquidise until the texture is quite smooth. Serve chilled in dessert glasses.

BREAKFAST MUESLI

The grains in this muesli are calming and focusing for the mind and body – the perfect way to start the detox day! Make sure that you purchase sun-dried rather than sulphur-dried fruits.

3 parts wheat flakes
1 part wheatgerm
4 parts millet flakes
1 part flaked almonds
1 part sunflower seeds
1 part dried apple
1 part dried pear

You can make up as much muesli in advance as you wish, and keep it in an airtight container.

fresh banana
soya milk

Serve with soya milk, topped with the fresh fruit. Soak the muesli in the soya milk for 10–20 minutes before serving.

DESSERTS and DRINKS

BANANA AND CASHEW SLICE

Bananas are anti-fungal and are a natural antibiotic. They detoxify by encouraging the production of the beneficial bacteria in the intestinal tract. Nuts are generously packed with an abundance of vitamins and minerals. They are high in protein and essential fatty acids, which are required for most bodily functions.
Makes 8 slices

Preheat the oven to 190°C/375°F/gas mark 5.

4 tablespoons sunflower oil
250g (9oz) bananas
$^1/_2$ teaspoon vanilla essence
1 teaspoon ground cinnamon
$^1/_4$ teaspoon ground cardamom

Blend in a liquidiser or food processor.

50g (2oz) cashew nuts

Add and blend for a few seconds to break them up.

50g (2oz) dessicated coconut
50g (2oz) oats
1 apple, peeled and grated

Add and blend for a few seconds.

Turn into a greased 23cm (9in) baking tin. Bake in the centre of the oven for 25–30 minutes. Leave to cool, then cut into wedges.

MILLET AND APRICOT PUDDING

Apricots are bursting with antioxidants, which have been shown to prevent cholesterol build-up in the arteries. Millet is an alkaline grain that is beneficial for combating stress. Serves 2

Preheat oven to 180°C/350°F/gas mark 4.

125g (4¹/₂ oz) millet

Toast in a dry frying pan over a medium heat, until it begins to change colour and give off a nutty aroma.

100ml (3¹/₂ fl oz) apple juice
100ml (3¹/₂ fl oz) orange juice
200ml (7fl oz) water

Add to the pan, cover and simmer for 30 minutes until the millet is soft and the mixture the consistency of porridge. You may need to add more water to prevent it from drying out.

4 fresh apricots, stoned and roughly chopped
1 tablespoon honey
100ml (3¹/₂ fl oz) soya milk
Pinch of ground cinnamon
1 tablespoon honey

Stir into the pan, then turn into an ungreased ovenproof dish with a lid. Place in the centre of the oven for 30 minutes.

25g (1oz) flaked almonds

Place on a baking sheet and toast under a medium grill until golden brown.

Honey, to serve

Serve the pudding hot, topped with the almonds and a little honey.

POACHED PEARS WITH HONEY AND PISTACHIOS

Poaching pears brings out their pectin content. Pectins bond to toxins and cholesterol in the body to facilitate their elimination. Pistachios cleanse the blood and are a tonic for the liver and kidneys. Serves 2

300ml (¹/₂ pint) water
3 tablespoons honey
¹/₂ cinnamon stick
1 clove
1 vanilla pod or ¹/₂ capful vanilla essence
Juice of ¹/₂ lemon
Juice of ¹/₂ orange

Heat in a pan just big enough to stand the pears in – they should be covered by the syrup.

2 large plump pears, peeled and cored but left whole

Poach without boiling for 10–15 minutes until soft. The required time will depend on the ripeness of the pears. Remove the pears and reserve. Reduce the syrup until quite thick, then remove from the heat and cool.

1 tablespoon chopped, unsalted pistachios, to decorate

Put pears on serving dishes and cover with the syrup. Decorate and serve.

STRAWBERRY AND RASPBERRY CHEESECAKE

Strawberries eliminate harmful toxins from the blood, making them ideal as a skin-cleansing food. Raspberries have an astringent quality, which helps to clear mucus and catarrh. They also help to relieve the pain of excess menstrual flow and muscle cramp. Serves 2

250g (9oz) low fat, low sugar oat biscuits

Place in a food processor and process to a fine crumb.

85g (3oz) soya margarine

Melt in a pan then add to the biscuits and process briefly. Press the mixture into a 25.5cm (10in) flan ring and refrigerate for 20 minutes to set.

570g (1¼ lb) silken tofu
1 teaspoon vanilla essence

Place in a liquidiser or food processor, and blend until smooth.

2 tablespoons concentrated strawberry and apple juice or raspberry and apple or rice syrup
⅛ teaspoon powdered agar agar

Heat the liquid in a pan and add the agar agar. Bring to a gentle simmer, stirring continuously until the grainy texture of the agar agar disappears. Add to the tofu and blend together. Pour immediately over the biscuit base and spread evenly. Refrigerate for 15 minutes to set.

220g (½ lb) of all fruit (no sugar or sweetener) jam

Heat in a pan until melted and pour evenly over the cheesecake.

125g (4½ oz) fresh strawberries and raspberries, mixed

Arrange on top and leave until cooled and set.

STRAWBERRY AND RASPBERRY SMOOTHIE

The acid and vitamin C in these fruits helps to cleanse the body of toxins. These red berries also help to relieve the symptoms of conditions that affect the urinary system, such as painful urination or the inability to urinate. Serves 1

10 raspberries
6 strawberries
1 banana
Juice of 1 orange
10 ice cubes

Blend well in a liquidiser and serve immediately.

APPLE, PEAR AND MINT JUICE

Research shows that these fruits can actually remove radioactive residue and toxic heavy metals from the digestive system. Apples and pears are excellent sources of pectin – a water-soluble fibre that binds to toxins in the system and helps their excretion from the body. Mint has a calming effect on digestion, protecting against stomach gas and destroying internal parasites. Makes 1 large glass

2 apples	Choose your favourite varieties of apples and pears, quarter them and
2 pears	push them through a juicing machine along with the mint. Serve
3–4 stems of fresh mint	immediately.

MELON, PEAR AND CELERY JUICE

Melon removes toxins while re-hydrating the body with its highly alkaline mineral content. It requires little digestion and passes through the system quickly. Celery reduces acid build-up and purifies the bloodstream. The iodine content in pears helps to regulate the body's metabolism. Pears are also high in fibre, which makes this juice a good tonic for clearing obstructed bowels. Makes 1 large glass

½ honeydew melon	Push through a juicing machine.
3 pears	
1 stick celery	
10 ice cubes	Place in a liquidiser or food processor, add the juice and blend together. Serve immediately.

CANTALOUPE MELON WITH ORANGE AND MINT

Melon and orange juice require little digestion, so are ideal if you need a quick energy-boost. Melons are high in silica and nutrients that tone and insulate the nerve fibres. Mint contains menthol, which enhances digestion and has an antispasmodic effect that eases digestive pain. Makes 1 large glass

1 cantaloupe melon, halved and seeded	Place the halves in serving bowls.
1 orange, peeled, thinly sliced and cut into quarters **Juice of 1 orange** **10 mint leaves, finely chopped**	Mix in a bowl. Pile the mixture into the melon halves and pour over any remaining juice. Serve chilled.

BANANA AND MANGO SMOOTHIE

Bananas are beneficial for dry conditions in the body, such as dry coughs and tight sensations in the chest. Mangoes have an immense blood-cleansing capacity that counteracts acidity and reduces the heat brought on by fever. Makes 1 large glass

2 bananas **½ mango** **15 ice cubes** **Juice of 1 orange**	Place in a food processor or liquidiser and blend until very smooth. Serve in a chilled glass.

index

bibliography

Kloss, J., *Back to Eden*, Back to Eden Publishing Co., 1992
McKeith, G., *Living Food for Health*, Piatkus, 2000
Onstadt, D., *Wholefoods Companion*, Chelsea Green, 1996
Pitchford, P., *Healing with Wholefoods*, North Atlantic Books, 1993

acknowledgments

Louisa J Walters would like to thank Lawrence and Sarah Dawkin-Jones, Will Hancock and Chris Rollinson for helping to test out recipes.
Aliza Baron Cohen would like to thank Alexis, Helen and all her family for their support and encouragement, and the (unborn) baby for inspiration.
Adrian Mercuri would like to thank his parents Antonio and Marisa and his brothers Jeff, Daniel and Renato for all their love and support.

bliss creative health centre

can be contacted at:
333 Portobello Road
London W10 5SA
tel: 020 8969 3331